THE
UNITY OF ISAIAH

A Study in Prophecy

By

OSWALD T. ALLIS

These things said Isaiah, because he saw his glory
and spake of him

Wipf and Stock Publishers
150 West Broadway • Eugene OR 97401
2000

The Unity of Isaiah
A Study in Prophecy
By Allis, Oswald T.

ISBN: 1-57910-550-5

Reprinted by *Wipf and Stock Publishers*
150 West Broadway • Eugene OR 97401

Previously published by Presbyterian and Reformed Publishing

CONTENTS

PREFACE

During a visit to the Harz Mountains, the writer heard this story told in a little gathering of ministers. A certain student for the ministry was told by his professor at the University, that no scholars any longer believed that Isaiah the contemporary of Hezekiah wrote the last twenty-seven chapters of the book that bears his name, that it was the unanimous judgment of scholars that these chapters were written by a prophet who lived toward the close of the Babylonian Captivity, more than a century after Isaiah's time. But it was also impressed upon him that when he was ordained and entered upon the work of the pastorate, he must tell his people that all the sixty-six chapters of this book were from the pen of Isaiah the contemporary of Hezekiah. The result was that when the young man, having been ordained and installed, entered the pulpit to preach his first sermon, he chose a text from Isa. 40-66 and again and again in the course of the sermon instructed his hearers that Isaiah the contemporary of Hezekiah uttered those words at the close of the Babylonian Captivity! The story has its humorous side; and it was largely for this reason that it was told on the occasion referred to. But it provides food for serious reflection. It shows very clearly the confusion and mental indigestion which is likely to follow the attempt to combine and assimilate incompatible and mutually exclusive ideas. This young man was to believe one thing for himself; he was to tell the flock of which he had just been made the spiritual shepherd another thing. Small wonder that, having in his very first discourse fallen "into a place where two seas met," he was in serious danger of making both intellectual and moral shipwreck.

In the more than forty years that have elapsed since the above incident, the situation has changed radically in one respect, in another it has remained the same. It has remained the same to this extent, that the higher critics never were more firmly convinced than they are today that the Unity of Isaiah has been completely disproved and the issue finally disposed of. It has changed in this respect, that those who have accepted this and other "assured results" of Criticism no longer think it necessary to camouflage their opinions or to conceal them from the laity. Rather are they concerned, now that they have gained positions of leadership and control in many religious bodies, to use every means in their power to convince every one of the correctness of those critical views which they now boldly advocate. The consequence is that many thoughtful and earnest Christians are today in a position somewhat similar to that of the young minister of our story. Their Bible tells them quite definitely that there are sixty-six chapters in "Isaiah." They may or may not be aware that the headings are no part of the Biblical text. But the introductory heading, "The Book of the Prophet Isaiah" certainly seems merely to summarize the statement in Isa. 1:1; and the page heading "Isaiah," which stands at the top of the pages containing chapters 40-66 just as it does in the case of chapters 1-39, seems to find clear support in, for example, the words of John 12:37-41. Yet they are told by these religious leaders, told with the utmost assurance and positiveness, that the theory of but one Isaiah is no longer held by competent scholars. Is it any wonder that they are confused and bewildered? Is it any wonder that they are tempted to leave Isaiah and many other parts of the Bible severely alone? Is it any wonder that Bible study is not on the increase but decidedly on the decrease in many circles in the Christian Church?

The aim of this brief study of a vitally important subject is to direct the attention of the reader to two very significant facts. The first is, that the only adequate and satisfactory explanation of the until recently all but universally accepted belief that Isaiah wrote the entire book which bears his name is to be found in the fact that such a belief is fully in accord with the teachings of the entire Bible as to the nature of prophecy and also with its teachings as to Isaiah and his writings. Were such not the case, it would be difficult if not impossible to account for this remarkable unanimity in accepting the unity of Isaiah, which continued for so many centuries. The second matter which also deserves very careful consideration is the fact that the rejection of the unity of Isaiah, which has become an essential dogma of the higher criticism, is primarily and mainly due to the acceptance by the critics of a theory as to the nature of prophecy which makes belief in the unity of Isaiah impossible. This modern theory proceeds on the assumption that prediction of the distant future is impossible, that the predictive element in prophecy is to be reduced to the minimum, and that the prophet is to be thought of as a man of his own day and age, who spoke to the people of his own day of matters of urgent and immediate concern to them. When the emphasis is thus placed on the contemporary scene and the distant future is minimized or ignored, an Isaiah who in the days of Hezekiah and the Assyrian peril could speak and did speak of a distant Babylonian Captivity and of Cyrus as the deliverer from it, becomes an anomaly, an absurdity, a living anachronism.

It is easy for the critics to draw a picture which is a caricature
of the Isaiah whom the Church for centuries believed to be the real
Isaiah and to contrast him, as an impossible visionary, with their
very human Isaiah who was a man of his age, vitally concerned
with the immediate problems of his contemporaries, with their
every day affairs and their pressing national problems. But it is
important to remember that while such a conception of the prophet
and of his role in Bible history must effectually destroy the unity
of Isaiah, it must also go far beyond this. It must also destroy
the entire fabric of Messianic prophecy. For an Isaiah who was
engrossed with and limited to the concerns of the present and
unable to foresee events lying a century and more in the future,
the Captivity and Cyrus, certainly could not be expected to have
any thing to say about that Coming One whose advent was even
more remote, more than half a millennium beyond the days of
Cyrus. When the scope of prophecy is so restricted that the element
of prediction is largely or wholly eliminated from the Bible, the
glorious predictions of the coming of Messiah in His First Advent
can no longer be regarded as Messianic and it cannot be said of
any of the Old Testament prophets, "he spoke of Him." These
predictions must have referred to events in the Old Testament
period and have been fulfilled in them. It follows inevitably also
from this theory of prophecy that the no less glorious predictions
of the New Testament which look forward to the Second Advent
of the Messiah must be explained and gotten rid of in similar
fashion. For these "exceeding great and precious promises" are
all *predictions* and many of them relate to things which, as history
has shown, were and even now may be "a great while to come."
Yet they are the confident hope of the Christian because they are
a sure word of prophecy, uttered by Him who said, "heaven and
earth shall pass away but my word shall not pass away" or by
His servants to whom He gave authority to speak in His name.
But if predictive prophecy, prophecy dealing with the distant future, is to be eliminated from the Bible, all of these precious
promises will perish with it; and the Christian who has believed
them will be of all men most miserable. Consequently, while the
question of the Unity of Isaiah is important in and of itself, it
becomes doubly important when we examine it in connection with
the theory of prophecy which is responsible for its rejection.

September 6, 1950   O. T. A.

FOREWORD

by

CLARENCE EDWARD MACARTNEY, LL.D., Litt.D.
Minister of the First Presbyterian Church, Pittsburgh, Pa.

When one takes up a book on a serious, difficult, and important subject like this, the Unity of Isaiah, the first thing one wants to know is "What are the qualifications of the author for the writing of such a book?" This book has for its author one eminently qualified to discuss the great subject with which it deals. Dr. Oswald T. Allis, son of a noted Philadelphia surgeon, is a graduate of the University of Pennsylvania, holds a Master's Degree from Princeton University, and was graduated from Princeton Theological Seminary in 1905. He pursued his graduate studies at the University of Berlin, which conferred upon him the degree of Doctor of Philosophy. For nineteen years he was on the staff at Princeton Theological Seminary, serving first as an instructor and then as assistant professor of Semitic Philology. For twelve years he was the able editor of the *Princeton Theological Review,* and for seven years was Professor of Old Testament and Exegesis at Westminster Theological Seminary, Philadelphia. Through the years he has contributed articles to Biblical and theological magazines and journals. This book is by no means his first venture in the field of Biblical authorship, for, in addition to *The Unity of Isaiah,* he is the author of *Prophecy and the Church, Bible Numerics, The Five Books of Moses,* and *Revision or New Translation?* Therefore, when we read the pages of *The Unity of Isaiah,* we realize at once that we are listening to a man who knows whereof he speaks.

The attempt of not a few Old Testament scholars to break up the book of Isaiah into fragments from different ages and different authors is, as Dr. Allis clearly points out at the beginning of his book, in keeping with a policy of Old Testament interpretation which denies the supernatural and robs the Old Testament prophecies of practically all predictive elements.

Prophecy and miracles were for ages considered the two great pillars of Christian truth and evidence. The tendency today has been to discount and undermine both of these pillars of evidence. It is to be remembered, however, that the fulfillment of prophecy is the one great evidence to which the Bible itself points. It is the argument of Christ about himself. It was the one great argument of the apostles for the authority and deity of Jesus Christ when they went forth to preach the Gospel. The argument from prophecy is that if we have a series of predictions foretelling clearly and closely future events which no native shrewdness and no clever guess could have arrived at and the fulfillment of which could not have been contrived by an impostor, then the fulfillment of such predictions necessitates a supernatural power at work. In other words, the fulfillment of prophecy proves that Christianity is a divine revelation. As Justin Martyr, who himself was converted to the Christian faith by a study of the prophets, put it, "To declare a thing shall come to pass long before it is in being, and then to bring it to pass, this or nothing is the work of God." It is not strange that the fine mind of Pascal saw in the fulfillment of the prophecies the strongest of all the evidences for Christianity. In his celebrated *Thoughts* he writes; "The greatest of the proofs of Jesus Christ are the prophecies. They are also what God has most provided for, for the event which has fulfilled them is a miracle which has subsisted from the birth of Christ even to the end." Those who believe that what Peter said to the Roman centurion, Cornelius, is true—"to Him give all the prophets witness," will have their faith strengthened by Dr. Allis' book on Isaiah.

Chapter III on *The Unity of the Book of Isaiah* is one of the most important and convincing in Dr. Allis' book. It is well known that according to the critical theories which have gained considerable recognition in the Church, the last twenty-seven chapters of the Book of Isaiah, or chapters 40 to 66, are assigned to the time of the Exile. Who the author of this great section of the Book of Isaiah was, no one knows, nor pretends to know. Neither the Old Testament nor the New Testament know anything of him. He remains, as Dr. Allis points out, the "Great Unknown." To speak of a Second Isaiah, and as some now do, of a Third Isaiah, has, Dr. Allis says, "no more significance than the x and y of an algebraic equation. They are merely symbols for unknowns, the value of which is still to be determined."

All students of the Bible were greatly stirred by the report of the discovery in 1947 in a cave in the Judean hills near the Dead Sea of an ancient "Isaiah Scroll." With few exceptions, paleographic experts who have examined the scroll are agreed that it is very old. Competent scholars assign it to about 150 B. C. If this is correct, then this Isaiah Scroll, discovered just three years ago, is by a thousand years the earliest manuscript of an entire book of the Hebrew Old Testament.

Everywhere the question was asked, "Will this ancient scroll confirm the critical theory of two, three, or even more Isaiahs?" It certainly does not. Dr. Allis points out that chapter 40 begins on the very last line of the column which contains chapters 38:9 to 39:8. The last words on the one column are, "Cry unto her," and the first words on the next column are, "that her warfare is accomplished." Certainly, therefore, the scribe who wrote this ancient manuscript of the prophecy was altogether unaware of what the critics alleged, that beginning with chapter 40 we have an important change of historical situation and an entire change in authorship.

If there was another Isaiah who wrote chapters 40 to 66, then he is, in many respects, a greater prophet than Jeremiah, Ezekiel, Daniel, or Zechariah. And yet, an altogether unknown prophet and author! This, as Dr. Allis points out, is "extremely unlikely, to say the least. It also lacks historical evidence to support it."

The paragraph by Dr. Allis on the New Testament and the unity of the Book of Isaiah is striking and convincing. In the New Testament Isaiah is quoted by name twenty times, which is more frequently than all the other "writing prophets" taken together. It is important, too, to note that in the books where Isaiah is quoted most frequently, the citations are made from *both* parts of the book. Matthew quotes Isaiah by name, three times from the first part and three times from the second. Paul in Romans quotes Isaiah five times by name, and from both parts of the book. Very striking, too, is the fact that St. John, chapter 12:38, cites, first, Isaiah 53:1, and then Isaiah 6:10, in consecutive verses as "Isaiah." From all this it is clear beyond any peradventure of a doubt that none of the New Testament writers had the slightest idea that the name Isaiah had any doubtful or ambiguous meaning, or that there was more than one prophet who was the author of the passages which they quote.

The impression one gets from the reading of the pages of Dr. Allis' calm and scholarly book is that if the question of whether there was one author of Isaiah, or two, or three, or more, were brought up in a court of law, the case of those who claim several authors for this sublime prophecy would quickly be thrown out of court for lack of evidence.

Devout Christians will not forget that our Lord, who began his ministry by quoting the beautiful passage from Isaiah 61, beginning, "The Spirit of the Lord is upon me," in the same night in which he was betrayed (Luke 22:37) quoted the words of the 53rd chapter of Isaiah, "And he was numbered with the transgressors," and said that that prediction would now be fulfilled in him and in his coming death. Nor will devout Christians forget the fact that when Philip the Evangelist got up into the chariot and found the Ethiopian Eunuch reading from the 53rd chapter of Isaiah the words, "He was led as a sheep to the slaughter, and like a lamb dumb before his shearers, so opened he not his mouth," and the Eunuch asked Philip whether the prophet was speaking of himself or some other man, he "opened his mouth and began at the same scripture, and preached unto him Jesus." (Acts 8:34, 35)

The question of the unity of the Book of Isaiah cannot be separated from the question of its witness to and its prediction of the work of Christ as our Redeemer. All those who believe that the Book of Isaiah predicts the birth, the good works and miracles, the shameful death, the resurrection, and the grand and final triumph of Christ, when he shall "divide the spoil with the strong" and shall "see of the travail of his soul and shall be satisfied," will find solid ground for their belief and their hope in this timely and most notable book by Dr. Allis. The whole Christian world is indebted to him.

The preparation of this special edition of *The Unity of Isaiah* and its presentation to the pastors in the Presbyterian Church in the U. S. A. has been made possible through the generous gift of a layman who is greatly concerned about the attitude of the Protestant Church toward the authority and inspiration of the Scriptures.

CHAPTER I

PROPHECY ACCORDING TO THE CRITICS

The student of history is well aware that the sceptical and decidedly hostile attitude toward the Supernatural which is so prevalent today is of relatively recent date, being largely the result of the "empirico-scientific" world-view which so powerfully influences and even controls the thinking of the "modern" man.[1] Miracle and prophecy were formerly quite generally regarded by Christians as furnishing conspicuous, even irrefutable, proof of the truth and divine authority of the Christian religion. They have now come to be regarded in many circles, even professedly Christian, as constituting the great and even the insuperable obstacle to the acceptance of Biblical Christianity by the scientifically trained man and woman of today.[2] Consequently, a vigorous and persistent effort has been made to eliminate the supernatural from the Bible, or at least to minimize its importance and to ignore it as much as possible. In text-books which represent the "critical" or "higher critical" viewpoint it is regarded as a matter of prime importance to *explain* the supernatural, which often means to *explain it away*, and to deal with the Bible in such a way that the supernatural will really cease to be *super*natural. The seriousness of this attempt cannot be exaggerated. For it is not too much to say that "by its own claim the Christian religion must stand or fall with the reality of the Supernatural. . . . It presents itself to us, not as an evolution of the divine in nature, but as a direct revelation of and from God, who, though in nature, was alone before it and is also distinct from it and above it."[3] In a word, to get rid of the Supernatural in Christianity is to get rid of Christianity. For Christianity is supernatural in its very essence. The simplest and most obvious illustration of this is prayer. Prayer is either communion with God, the human soul having intercourse with the God who made it, or it is merely a spiritual

---

[1] See the chapter on "Christianity and the Supernatural" in S. G. Craig, *Christianity Rightly So Called* (1946), pp. 89-111.

[2] Examples of this attitude are Millar Burrows, *An Outline of Biblical Theology* (Westminster Press, 1946), pp. 16-18, 130-132 and R. H. Pfeiffer, *An Introduction to the Old Testament* (Harper, 1941), p. 755. Both of these scholars regard miracle and predictive prophecy as a definite liability to Christianity.

[3] W. B. Greene, Jr., Article "The Supernatural" in *Biblical and Theological Studies* by the Faculty of Princeton Theological Seminary (1912) pp. 144f.

exercise, a form of auto-suggestion, which is not converse with Another, but a kind of pious soliloquy.

The attitude of which we have been speaking is particularly plain in the attempts which have been made to eliminate *prediction* from *prophecy*.[4] One of the most influential of the advocates of this new conception of prophecy, the late professor A. B. Davidson of Edinburgh, described the function of the Hebrew prophet in the following terms: "The prophet is always a man of his own time and it is always to the people of his own time that he speaks, not to a generation long after, nor to us. And the things of which he speaks will always be things of importance to the people of his own day, whether they be things belonging to their internal life and conduct, or things affecting their external fortunes as a people among other peoples."[5] While this definition, as we may call it, does not deny the possibility of predictive prophecy, it tends quite obviously to minimize, if not to eliminate from it, the definitely predictive. If the prophet is "always a man of his own time," it will be natural to suppose that his viewpoint and horizon will be largely or entirely those of his own time. If he always addresses "the people of his own time" and always speaks to them of "things of importance" to them, the tendency will be to limit the scope of prophecy to the immediate concerns and the pressing interests of the people among whom the prophet lives, and to make his message deal only very sketchily, if at all, with the far horizons of the future. He will speak as a contemporary to his contemporaries. The "Thus saith the Lord," with which the prophet introduces his message and which asserts its divine source and authority, and the "Behold the days come," with which it reaches out into the dim and distant future, will tend to have little more meaning than the "In my judgment, this is what the present situation calls for" of the far-seeing statesman and the zealous preacher of righteousness. The advocates of this new conception of prophecy claim that it makes the prophets real human beings, personalities, men of flesh and blood, dealing with the vital problems of their day, instead of mere mouthpieces, colorless automatons, rapt mystics, who lived in another world from that in which their lot was actually cast. Were this all, it might simply mean that they have emphasized a side of prophecy which some over-zealous students of prophecy have been inclined to ignore or neglect. But the further and disastrous result of this "humanizing" of the prophets is that the "man of God"

---

[4] See Appendix I.

[5] *Hastings Dictionary of the Bible*, iv., p. 118b.

tends very definitely according to their teaching to become, however specially gifted, merely a "man among men."

How strongly Davidson's definition tends to minimize the predictive element in prophecy is indicated by another statement: ". . . prophecy is not identical with *prediction*. Prediction is the least element in it. I do not know that it is an essential element in it at all; though I should hesitate to affirm that it is not, because almost all, if not all, of the prophets in the remains which we possess of their literary activity do give predictions."[6] This statement makes it quite clear that Davidson was strongly inclined to regard as unimportant and unessential a feature of prophecy which on his own admission is to be found in practically every prophetical book of the Old Testament.[7] Even a cursory survey of the "critical" discussions of Prophecy that have appeared within recent years should make it abundantly plain to everyone that Alexander, writing a century ago, correctly defined the attitude which has characterized the critical movement from its beginning, when he said: "The successive writers of this modern school, however they may differ as to minor points among themselves, prove their identity of principle by holding that *there cannot be distinct prophetic foresight of the distant future.*"[8]

Now if, as Davidson was almost prepared to maintain, the element of prediction, at least as it concerns the distant future, forms no essential part in Biblical prophecy, the question immediately arises, How are the many predictions in the Bible which speak of such a future to be accounted for; and how are they to be dealt with to bring them into harmony with this assumption of the critics?

There are several ways in which this desired result can be accomplished. The first is to change the *situation* of the prophecy. If according to the Biblical record a certain prophecy was uttered many years before the event occurred which is elsewhere described as its fulfilment, or if it definitely refers to a far distant event, it can be alleged that, since prophecy cannot deal with a "non-existent situation," the prediction must really have been uttered much later than is stated, shortly before (or even after!) the event to which it refers. Or, if the situation as given in the Biblical record seems to be a suitable one for some such utterance as is recorded, it may be alleged that the prediction

---

[6] *Old Testament Prophecy,* p. 11.

[7] Appendix II.

[8] J. A. Alexander, *The Earlier Prophecies of Isaiah* (1846), p. xxxviii. See Appendix III.

did not originally refer to a far distant event, that it was a general, vague, and indefinite utterance which dealt primarily with current or proximate events, and that the long range and precise fulfilment are the result of later editing, amplifying, or revising of the prophecy by writers who for various reasons wished to give special importance to these later events, by representing them as the fulfilment of ancient prediction.[9] In this way the predictive element can be largely or wholly eliminated from the prophecy and attributed to tradition, legend, pious imagination and the like. The result is the same in either case. Either by changing the *situation*[10] of the prophecy or by reducing its *scope* and the definiteness of its reference to future events, the predictive element can be largely made to disappear from Old Testament prophecy. And this is brought about on and justified by the *assumption* that predictive prophecy in the Biblical sense of the word is impossible and that the data of Scripture which so clearly teach the contrary must be brought into harmony at whatever cost with this basic principle cf critical interpretation. The following examples will serve to show how this result is obtained by the critics, and also how seriously these methods to which they must resort undermine the credibility and trustworthiness of the Biblical record.

MAKING THE EVIDENCE FIT THE THEORY

Genesis 15:13, "and they shall afflict them four hundred years." Here almost at the very beginning of patriarchal history we meet with a revelation which quite obviously deals with the remote future. Its situation was sometime during the first ten years of Abram's sojourn in Canaan and before he married Hagar (16:3); and its scope covers a period of at least 400

---

[9] J. M. Powis Smith ("The Study of the O. T. and of the Religion of Israel" in *A Guide to the Study of the Christian Religion,* 1916) asserts that "the history of Hebrew literature . . . is a history of revisions" (p. 152). This is and must be the assumption which underlies and supposedly justifies those "dissectings" and "emendings" of the text which are to anyone who has any regard for the authority of Scripture a major indictment of the Higher Criticism.

[10] In recent years, owing to the popularity of Form Criticism (*Gattungsgeschichte*) much attention has been given to the "situation in life" (*Sitz im Leben*) of various types and patterns of Biblical literature, with a view to noting their distinctive features and tracing their history and origin. But the emphasis on *situation* as the key to the understanding of prophecy is of much earlier date. It goes back to the very beginning of the critical interpretation of Prophecy, especially as it is involved in the question of the unity of Isaiah. This is indicated by Alexander's remark that one of the main objections to the unity of Isaiah is "the assumption that the local and historical allusions of a prophet must be always those of his own time" (*The Later Prophecies of Isaiah* (1847) p. xix). See Appendix III.

years.[11] How do the critics bring such a prediction into accord with their theory that prophecy always deals with the present or the immediate future? They find a simple solution of the difficulty in their theory as to the origin and date of the Pentateuch. According to the view most generally held by them, none of the documents of which they believe the Pentateuch to be composed dates from earlier than the 9th century B.C. (a thousand years or more later than Abraham's time). They hold that the particular documents (J and E) of which this chapter was composed were not combined until about 650 B.C., that the latest of the sources (P) dates from a couple of centuries later, and that the final editing of the Pentateuch was not completed until about 450 B.C. Hence, for those who hold that these documents are all many centuries later than the time of Abraham and that they were *edited, revised,* and *redacted* in process of time, it is both natural and easy to argue or simply assert that the "prediction" to Abram was "colored" by the actual course of subsequent events. Thus, a prominent critic has even suggested that, since the late writer (P) records as a fact of history that the sojourn in Egypt was "430 years" (Ex. 12:40), the final editor may have inserted in Gen. 15:13 the words "400 years."[12] Thus the development might have been as follows; the oldest document (J) says nothing about a sojourn in a strange land, the next one (E) speaks of such a sojourn and of a return in the fourth generation (v. 16), the final editor or redactor inserts the words, "and they shall serve them 400 years," and he does it on the basis of the record of the fulfilment given in the latest document (P).[13] This is of course equivalent to saying that the remarkable scope and definiteness of the prediction in Gen. 15:13 is simply due to the reading back into it of the record of its fulfilment. The actual *situation* of the prediction in the form in which it stands in Gen. 15:13 is thus placed later than the event which *fulfils* it! It becomes a prophecy *post eventum.* Obviously those who are prepared to accept such an explanation of the prophecy have no reason to be troubled or disconcerted

---

[11] We need not concern ourselves here with the difficult and much debated question whether the 400 years, which are more exactly defined in Ex. 12:41 as 430 years refer only to the length of the sojourn in Egypt (the Long Chronology) or include the prior sojourn of the patriarchs in the land of Canaan (the Short Chronology). On either interpretation, the prophecy, since it deals with a period which extends at least four centuries into the unknown future, is definitely predictive.

[12] Peake's *Commentary on the Bible,* p. 150. The notes on Genesis are by the editor.

[13] See Skinner's discussion of Gunkel's analysis of chap. 15 in his Commentary on Genesis in the *Internat. Crit. Series,* p. 277.

by the fact that it refers to a distant future. The prediction
in its original form, if indeed there was such a prediction at all,
may have been vague and indefinite and have referred to a
proximate event such as Abraham's brief sojourn in Gerar.
Dextrous manipulation of the evidence can produce surprising
results! Gen. 46:1-4 must of course be similarly treated.

Genesis 49 contains a prediction regarding "the last days"
uttered by the patriarch Jacob. It concerns the future of his
sons and their descendants; and it was uttered by Jacob from
his deathbed (v. 33). That was the *situation* of the prophecy
according to the Biblical narrative. The critical interpretation
gives us quite a different situation. It is this: "The allusions
in the poem are to conditions in the period of the Judges,
Samuel, and David. The date of the composition, therefore, is
probably in the 10th century B.C."[14] Since the death of David
took place rather early in the 10th century, a "composition"
dating from the middle of that century which dealt with "conditions" in the time of David and earlier would not really deal
with the future at all. There would not need to be any prediction
in it. For its situation would be determined by the actual course
of the *historical* events which it records. The fact that these
events are described as *future* and represented as *pre*dicted by
Jacob would then mean either that the author simply put them
into the mouth of the patriarch with a view to giving them
added authority, or that he edited or touched up an old prophecy, allegedly by Jacob, adding details which the critics now
recognize as evidencing its late date.

Deuteronomy 28 has, according to the context in which it
stands, a very striking and impressive situation. It forms part
of one of the memorable discourses delivered by Moses shortly
before his death to the generation of Israelites which was about
to enter in and possess the land which their fathers had failed
to gain because of disobedience and unbelief. It is full, therefore, of exhortation and warning for the future. Toward the end
of the chapter, the awful consequences of disobedience are portrayed with the utmost vividness (vss. 47-57). This utterance
has been dated by most critics from about the time of Josiah's
reform (622 B.C.). This reduces the prophetic perspective very
greatly, especially if the siege of Jerusalem by Nebuchadnezzar
is regarded as particularly referred to. For a contemporary
of Josiah might well imagine that Jerusalem would suffer the
same fate at the hands of the Chaldean kings of Babylon as
Samaria had suffered a century before at the hands of the war-

[14] *Westminster Study Edition of the Holy Bible* (1948), p. 85.

like Assyrian. But some critics go much further than this. According to one interpretation we have in these verses an *eye-witness* description of the actual siege of Jerusalem by Neb-uchadnezzar.[15] According to another it is the siege of Samaria by Shalmaneser and Sargon which is here portrayed.[16] This gives us three situations for the prophecy all of which are quite different from the Biblical one. The advocates of these three views differ among themselves as to the actual situation of the prophecy. But they are agreed in rejecting the situation assigned to it by the Bible (that it was uttered by Moses) ; and they are agreed in choosing situations which either reduce the predictive element very greatly or eliminate it completely.

1 Samuel 2 :1-10. Hannah concludes her prayer of thanksgiving and praise with the words: "And he shall give strength unto his king and exalt the horn of his anointed." This was prophetic. For it was Hannah's son Samuel, a mere child when she uttered these words, who was destined to be the "king maker," to anoint first Saul and then David to be king over Israel. We do not know how old Samuel was when he anointed Saul. Probably an interval of forty to fifty years lay between the prophecy and its first fulfilment. So we are told that, "It is generally agreed by critics that this psalm bears no relation to the circumstances of Samuel's birth, and that it cannot have been composed by Hannah. The reference to the king in v. 10 presupposes a later age than that of Hannah, and the whole tenor of the poem points to a more advanced stage of Hebrew thought, the leading idea being the sovereign power of Jehovah." The ascription to Hannah is explained as due to "a mistaken application of 1 :5*b* to the circumstances of Hannah."[17] In other words, according to the theory held by the critics as to the situation and scope of prophecy, Hannah could not have uttered the words which are ascribed to her. So the statement in 1 :5*b* is to be regarded as a *mistake*.

2 Samuel 7. This chapter contains the great Messianic prophecy regarding David's house, which has its fulfilment in Solomon and in the Messiah, "great David's greater Son." The occasion is definitely stated. It was David's desire to build a house for the

---

[15] R. H. Pfeiffer, *An Introduction to the Old Testament*, p. 184.

[16] A. C. Welch, *The Code of Deuteronomy*, pp. 57f., 193ff.; also *Deuteronomy, the Framework of the Code*, p. 204.

[17] *A New Commentary*, edited by Gore, Goudge, and Guillaume (1928), p. 218. Similarly we are told in the *Westminster Study Edition* regarding v. 10 "This suggests that a Messianic psalm of different origin has been used by the editor to express Hannah's exultation" (p. 373). If this was done by the "final" editor, the psalm might have been inserted as late as "between 650 and 530 B.C." (p. 369).

Lord, after the Lord had given him rest from his enemies. Nathan's prophecy speaks first of David's "seed," who shall build the house which David is not permitted to build, and then it goes on to speak of David's "house" and "kingdom" which are to continue "for ever." That this prophecy was uttered before the birth of Solomon is indicated by v. 12 (cf. 1 Chr. 22:9) and that it is intended as a prediction is obvious. But the view of the critics, as stated by one of them, is that it was "probably composed toward the close of the Jewish Monarchy by a writer of the Deuteronomic school. (Verse) 13, referring to Solomon and his Temple, is a later addition. This Divine promise of permanence to the Davidic dynasty is an early form of the Messianic Hope of Israel."[18] It will be noted that this writer is not content with claiming that the narrative was "composed" by a writer of the Deuteronomic school,[19] which makes it several centuries later than the time of David. He goes still further and treats v. 13 as "a later addition." This disposes of the *pre*diction regarding Solomon and the building of the temple. And the Messianic prediction in which, as David says, the Lord has spoken of His servant's house "for a great while to come" is spoken of as "an early form of the Messianic Hope of Israel." The use of the word "early" in speaking of a composition which according to the critics probably dates from "toward the close of the Jewish Monarchy" is significant because, as we have just seen, according to 1 Sam. 2, Hannah a generation before David's time prophesied concerning "the Anointed" (*Messiah*) of the Lord.

1 Kings 13. This prophecy regarding the altar at Bethel is given a very definite situation, the reign of Jeroboam the son of Nebat, probably soon after he instituted the calf-worship at Bethel (v. 1). An unnamed prophet declares "in the name of the Lord" that "a child shall be born unto the house of David,

[18] So W. H. Bennett, in *Peake's Commentary on the Bible*, p. 288. Similarly Driver in his *Introduction* included this chapter, as well as Hannah's Song, among the passages which he regarded as "relatively the latest" in the Books of Samuel (p. 183). Cf. Creelmann, *Introd* p. 77. According to Cornill, "the question is, whether this chapter is the root of Messianic prophecy or one of the latter's offshoots. Everything argues the latter alternative; it can hardly have been written before the time of Isaiah" (*Introd.*, p. 197).

[19] Cf. the discussion of Deut. 28 above. It is the view of the critics that a school of writers living about the time of Josiah composed the Book of Deuteronomy and represented it as Mosaic and also that they *edited* the books of Joshua, Judges, Samuel and Kings to make their statements accord with the teachings of Deuteronomy. This was, of course, a necessary further step because they had represented their "law book" as so ancient and claimed for it the authority of Moses. Consequently to the critics "Deuteronomic" is equivalent to non-Mosaic!

Josiah by name," who shall profane and destroy the altar at Bethel at which Jeroboam is now sacrificing. Jeroboam was the first king of the Northern Kingdom. Josiah was the last great king of the Southern Kingdom and came to the throne nearly a century after the last of Jeroboam's successors on the throne of Israel had passed away. Hence the mention of Josiah by name makes the element of prediction in this prophecy very striking. As to this we are told by the critics: "A prophet from Judah denounces Jeroboam's sanctuary at Beth-el and foretells its destruction. Since Josiah carried out this destruction, his name became attached to this prediction (2 Kgs. 23:17)."[20] Here the Biblical "situation" is accepted as correct. But the reference to Josiah by name is eliminated; and the predictive element is reduced to language which, it may seem to the critic, might have been uttered by any prophet or pious Israelite, who had a zeal for the true worship of the God of Israel and abhorred idolatry as an abomination which He would surely punish severely.[21]

2 Kings 10:28-31 contains the promise made to Jehu that his sons "of the fourth generation" should sit upon his throne. If, as seems probable, the situation of this prophetic utterance was early in Jehu's reign, it would have a scope of some eighty years. In any case it covered more than half a century, since the reign of Jeroboam II was about forty years in length. Consequently, we find that this passage is described as one of "the more important editorial (redactional) verses of different date" in 2 Kings.[22] If it is the work of the "Deuteronomic" redactor, who plays an important role in these books, according to the critics, it would represent a revision or insertion dating from

---

[20] *Westminster Study Edition,* pp. 468f. A more drastic method is simply to treat chap. 13 as "a prophetic legend of a highly grotesque sort" (Cornill, *Introduction,* p. 213) and declare it to be "a quite late production." Cf. Creelman, *Introduction,* p. 134. A special reason for this drastic treatment of 1 Kgs. 13 is, of course, that this prophecy has frequently been appealed to as furnishing a parallel, both in scope and definiteness to the Cyrus prophecy (Isa. 44:28) considered as an utterance of Isaiah, the son of Amoz.

[21] The mention of Josiah by name in this prophecy is not the only *definite* feature in it, although it is the one which has received the most attention and been most frequently challenged. The description of the method by which the defiling of the altar was to be accomplished is equally noteworthy. The "offering" (i.e., "sacrificing") of the priests of the high places on their own altars and the burning of dead men's bones on them to defile them are both unique features which are expressly referred to in II Kgs. 23:16, 20 as fulfilled by Josiah. In fact the phraseology of the latter passage in describing the fulfilment follows that of chap. 13 to a noticeable degree. Those who regard the naming of Josiah as suspicious and treat it as a later addition must go still further and eliminate these other equally precise features from the prophecy.

[22] Creelman, *Introduction,* p. 138.

about a century after the fall of the Northern Kingdom and about two centuries after the prophecy purported to have been made. This would make it easy to assert that an ancient tradition that Jehu's revolt was viewed with favor by the religious leaders of his time, was later worked up into a specific, long-range prediction, long after the event to which it referred had become a fact of history.

Psalm 45:6, "Thy throne, O God, is for ever and ever." We are told by the critics that this psalm "was composed in celebration of the marriage of one of Israel's kings," and that "these words are addressed to the king, who rules as God's representative." It is further pointed out that, "In most countries of the ancient East the kings were deified, but Israelite kings were not"—a statement of fact which is very important. "This address, however, follows the Eastern pattern." This is stated categorically despite the damaging admission which is immediately added: "There is no other example of this address in the O.T." So we are told: "Later this psalm was explained by Jewish interpreters as referring to the Messiah. Many Christians have also allegorized it in order to make it refer to Christ and the Church."[23] "Many Christians" must include, therefore, the writer of the Epistle to the Hebrews. For "Heb. 1:8, 9 applies this passage to Christ." So we are left to decide for ourselves whether such Jewish-Christian allegorizing has any warrant in fact! The *original* meaning, according to these critics, was that the writer in the extravagance and exuberance of poetic panegyric was extolling the Israelitish king and praising him as *divine!* And this style of courtly address, which is such a flagrant violation of the First Commandment and so inappropriate to any earthly king, is later *applied* in the Epistle to the Hebrews to the Divine Messiah! Nay more, it is appealed to as proof of His uniqueness!

Psalm 110:1. According to the heading, this psalm is Davidic, which means that it was composed within the lifetime of David the son of Jesse (cir. 1000 B.C.). This gives us its *situation* in general terms. In all three of the Synoptic Gospels we are told that Jesus quoted this verse, in an argument with the scribes and Pharisees, to prove that the Messiah, who is David's son, being also David's Lord, must be greater than his father David.

---

[23] *Westminster Study Edition,* pp. 738f. The comment on Heb. 1:7f. in the N. T. section of this handbook (p. 406) simply tells us that in vv. 5-14 "The Son's superiority is attested by a series of O. T. passages." Regarding vv. 8f. which quotes Ps. 45:6f. we are told that it attests "his righteous character." We are not told that it asserts his *Deity.* We could not expect this in view of the treatment of the psalm in the O. T. section.

The argument has three steps: that *David* uttered these words (all three Gospels assert this specifically), that in uttering them he spake by inspiration of the Holy Spirit, and that he was speaking of his "Son," the Messianic King who was to come of his house, and called him *Lord.* The whole point of the argument lies in the situation (authorship) of the words quoted: that it is David the king who speaks of his royal Descendant as greater than himself: "If David then call him Lord, how is he his son?" The critics have long maintained that only relatively few of the Psalms are Davidic, and that even those which may have been composed by him were more or less extensively edited in the course of time.[24] So they speak of this psalm as "popularly supposed to be by David and to refer to the Messiah," as "commonly thought to be written by David," and point out that "(the Jews) hold that David wrote Ps. 110:1 and regard it as Messianic"—all of which serves to indicate more or less definitely the view which they clearly hold, which is that "David may not have written Ps. 110."[25] Yet they argue that this does not affect "the point" of the argument which they hold to be "that the Messiah is Lord and no mere follower of another's pattern of leadership and rule."[26] This amounts to saying that the basis of the argument, the Davidic *authorship* of the psalm, the Davidic *situation* of the prophecy, can be questioned or denied, without affecting the validity of the conclusion, that David's Son must be greater than His father David.

Isaiah 7:8b, "and within threescore and five years shall Ephraim be broken, that it be not a people." With these words the prophet pronounces the final doom of the apostate Northern Kingdom. It has long been recognized that there were three steps in the fulfilment of this prediction: (1) the invasion of Tiglath-pileser who came to the aid of Ahaz against Rezin and Pekah and who greatly weakened the power of the Northern Kingdom by warfare and deportation (2 Kgs. 15:27-31; 16:7-9); (2) the capture of Samaria by Sargon in 722 B.C. (2 Kgs. 17:6); (3) the

---

[24] A thorough discussion of "The Headings of the Psalms" was published by Prof. R. D. Wilson in the *Princeton Theological Review* (1926), vol. xxiv, pp. 1-37, 353-395. His conclusion was: "As far as the objective evidence goes the headings of the psalms are presumptively correct" (p. 395).

[25] "May not" is so definitely an understatement that it sounds almost ironical, were it not obviously intended to avoid shocking the reader too much by a definite denial of Davidic authorship. Most critics are quite certain that David did not write this psalm.

[26] *Westminster Study Edition* (N. T. Section), pp. 60f., 100f., 154. The sentence which precedes the one just quoted is noteworthy: "V. 37 does not necessarily deny the Davidic descent of the Messiah, but insists that by his divine position and power the Messiah is the Lord of David as of all men" (p. 101).

repopulating of Samaria with foreigners by Esarhaddon (17:24; Ezra 4:2). The invasion of Judea by Rezin and Pekah which was the occasion of this prophecy took place about 734 B.C. The interval between this event and Esarhaddon's death in 669 B.C. is approximately 65 years. When Esarhaddon issued his edict we do not know. But it was within the 65 years of the prediction. So understood the prediction was fulfilled as Isaiah foretold; and the "breaking" of Samaria included and ended with the repeopling of the land by strangers. Yet many critics are prepared to insist that the fulfilment must be found in the fall of Samaria in 722 B.C. Some treat v. 8*b* as a gloss added by a later editor who was better acquainted with *history* than Isaiah and his contemporaries could have been and who knew of Esarhaddon's colonizing of Samaria.[27] Another explanation which is offered is that Isaiah simply overestimated the time required for the overthrow of the Northern Kingdom. So we are told: *"threescore and five.* Actually Ephraim, the Northern Kingdom, fell in 722/721 B.C., only twelve years after this prophecy."[28] The object of the "actually . . . only" is of course to make it very plain to the reader that the prophet Isaiah made a guess which missed the mark by more than half a century. To make such an inference appear inevitable, no mention is made of the possibility that the prophecy may properly include a reference to any event later than the fall of Samaria.

Isaiah 7:14. According to the critical theory regarding prophecy, the logical, we may even say the inevitable, interpretation of the Immanuel Prophecy has recently been stated very briefly as follows: "v. 14. *virgin.* The Hebrew word means a young woman old enough for marriage. The prediction is that nine months hence a mother will name her newborn son Immanuel ('God with Us') as an expression of faith that God is with his people to save them."[29] This is the entire comment on this verse. There is no intimation that the "prediction" is Messianic. It is to be fulfilled in nine months. When we turn to the comment on Matt. 1:23f. in the same volume we read: "v. 23. Cf. Isa. 7:14. *virgin.* The Hebrew word means 'young woman'; the Greek translation is followed here. The Isaiah verse, originally spoken of a birth in Isaiah's day, is here applied to Jesus' birth."[30] It is to be carefully noted that the commentators say "applied" not "fulfilled." There is a world of difference between

[27] Cf., Duhm, *Das Buch Jesaia*, 1902, p. 49.
[28] *Westminster Study Edition*, p. 936. Delitzsch traces this view back to Eichhorn.
[29] *Ibid.*, p. 936. See Appendix IV.
[30] *Ibid.*, p. 26 (N. T. Section).

the two words. Furthermore they do not tell us why it was so applied or whether such an application was legitimate or not. Their main desire seems to be to deny that Isaiah referred to a *virgin* birth; and they are not even prepared to insist that Matthew did.[31] Here we have, both in what is said and in what is left unsaid, the logical conclusions of the critical interpretation of prophecy: Isaiah referred to a perfectly natural and normal birth which was already in process of accomplishment when he spoke these words. Hence the only connection between it and the birth of Jesus, if there is any connection, must be found in the *analogy* between the two events. In a time of national peril and apostasy, Isaiah saw in the not at all improbable event that a young mother, with the faith and joyous anticipation which has characterized motherhood from the time of Eve, would give her newborn son the name "God with us," the proof that God had not forsaken and would not forsake his people. Similarly, seven centuries later, in a time of national peril another young mother, with similar hope and expectancy, calls her infant son, not Immanuel but a still more significant and precious name, Jesus ("The LORD is salvation"), as the expression of a similar faith. There is an analogy. Yes! but nothing we can call a *fulfilment*. And if the birth of Immanuel in Isaiah's time was a perfectly natural one, then analogy would clearly favor the rejection of the virgin birth of Jesus.[32]

[31] That such is the case is indicated by the following words contained in the notes to Matt. 1:18-25 in the *Westminster Study Edition*. "Jesus Christ was not merely a man who earned divine recognition. His birth was the result of the creative act of the living God who by his Spirit thus acted to give salvation to his people (v. 21). On any view of the birth of Jesus, this conviction of God's purposeful working is basic" (p. 25). The words, "on any view of the birth of Jesus," are significant. In their context they indicate quite plainly that the editors admit, and, in view of their insistence upon the meaning "young woman" instead of "virgin," that they prefer some other view of the birth of Jesus than that one which involves a virgin birth. This raises a vital question. Both Matthew and Luke tell us definitely that Joseph was the father of Jesus only by adoption. If Jesus was not "conceived by the Holy Ghost, born of the Virgin Mary," whose son was He?

[32] Thus Zenos, on the assumption that "the only admissible view" of the prophecy is that it refers to a birth in the prophet's own time, gives us the choice between two explanations of the use of the prophecy by Matthew: viz., that "the use of the passage by Matthew must be either the result of misunderstanding of the prophet's meaning, or the appropriation of his words as a formula in which the virgin birth of the Saviour might be felicitously embodied." He tells us that the evangelist may have expressed his thought of the meaning of the birth of Jesus by "applying the old oracle to the event he was narrating." And he adds, "Such an appropriation although not correct, judged by standards of modern literary and historical usage, would be in perfect harmony with the methods of using the O. T. at the time" (*New Standard Bible Dictionary*, p. 368b). Such an explanation speaks volumes. It not only denies the unique inspiration of the New Testament writers. It asserts that their standards of literary honesty were lower than our own.

Isaiah 9:6. The name of the child that is to be "given" to Israel appears in AV and RV as "Wonderful, Counsellor, the mighty God, the everlasting Father, the Prince of peace." According to this rendering, every one of these marvellous titles is to be borne by the Child that is here described. It is a glorious Messianic prophecy. Yet we are now being told that "The name given him may be translated, 'A wonderful counsellor is the mighty God, the Father of eternity, the Prince of peace'." In order that the full implication of this rendering may be appreciated by the reader, the explanation is added, "The Messiah's name describes the nature of the God for whom he is to rule."[33] This means that every one of these glorious titles and attributes is by this translation taken away from the Messiah and given to "the God for whom he is to rule." So understood, this name does not differ essentially from many other theophoric names in the O.T., which describe the character of the God of Israel and not the character of the person who bears the name. Such names as Elimelech (My God is king), Gedaliah (Jehovah is great), Jehoram (Jehovah is exalted) tell us nothing about the men who bore them, but only describe the character of the God whom they (supposedly) worshipped. In some cases these men were true to their names, like Elijah whose name, My God is Jehovah, was the very symbol and epitome of the mighty struggle at Carmel (1 Kgs. 18:39). In other cases their very names condemned them, or were falsified in meaning by their lives. Such was the case with both Jehoram of Israel and Jehoram of Judah; while Manasseh, who *forgot* the God of Israel and served Baal, gave to a name rich in historical significance (Gen. 41:51) a sinister meaning which made it synonymous with Apostate. Consequently, this new interpretation of the name of the Messiah empties it of all Messianic significance. It need not refer to Christ; and to call the prophecy Messianic, while at the same time emptying it of its richest and most precious meaning, is unworthy of the sober and careful scholar and indicates a definite anti-supernatural bias.[34]

Isaiah 13 contains an utterance which is specifically described as "the burden of Babylon, which Isaiah the son of Amoz did see." This heading assigns the utterance a situation in the Assyrian period and probably during the reign of Hezekiah. It refers to the overthrow of this great city by the Medes, a

---

[33] *Westminster Study Edition,* p. 939.

[34] For a defense of the traditional interpretation of this passage, see article, "The Child whose Name is Wonderful," by John D. Davis, in *Biblical & Theol. Studies,* by the Faculty of Princeton Theological Seminary, 1912, pp. 91-108.

disaster which certainly began with the capture of the city by the Medes and Persians in 538 B.C., but was not completed until a considerably later date. So we are told by the critics that "This *burden* or pronouncement of doom, upon Babylon, dates from the time when Media (v. 17) was threatening it, in the middle of the sixth century B.C."[35] This means that the heading of the prophecy (v. 1) is to be completely disregarded, and the utterance is to be assigned to a situation more than a century after Isaiah's time when the Median menace was clearly in view.[36]

Isaiah 39:5-7. The prediction that "sons," i.e., descendants of Hezekiah will be carried to Babylon can be dated fairly accurately. The occasion was the coming of the servants of Merodach-baladan to congratulate Hezekiah on his restoration to health and to inquire about the sign which had been given him (2 Chr. 32:31). This indicates a date or situation in about the middle of Hezekiah's reign for a prediction which was not fulfilled for more than a century. If the narrative comes to us from the pen of Isaiah himself, we have here a definite prediction of future events. But many critics prefer to take the view that chaps. 36-39 of Isaiah have been taken over from 2 Kings. This makes it possible to argue that the hand of the Deuteronomic redactor has been at work on this prediction.[37]

Micah 4:10. Here the Babylonian Captivity is clearly predicted by a prophet whose situation, according to 1:1, was not

[35] *Westminster Study Edition,* p. 945. Cf. p. 955 where a similar statement is made regarding chap. 21: "Prediction (not by Isaiah) that Babylon will be conquered by the Elamites and the Medes (cf. ch. 13). Babylon was taken by the Persians in 539 B.C."

[36] G. A. Smith denied the Isaianic authorship of chaps. 13-14:23, 24-27, 34-35, nearly eight chapters in the First Part of Isaiah, because he regarded them as "containing no reference to Isaiah himself nor to any Jewish king under whom he labored, and painting both Israel and the foreign world in quite a different state from that in which they lay during his lifetime." He says of chap. 13, "Only one of the prophecies in question confirms the tradition that it is by Isaiah, viz., chap. xiii., which bears the title, *Oracle of Babylon which Isaiah, the son of Amoz, did see.*" To meet this difficulty he remarks: "but titles are themselves so much the report of tradition, being of a later date than the rest of the text, that it is best to argue the question apart from them" (*Book of Isaiah,* ii. p. 403). In other words, if a passage has no heading or title, the critic is at liberty to determine its date solely on the basis of his view as to its probable situation. If it has a title, that title is to be ignored if it conflicts with the critic's decision as to the situation. It is this arbitrary treatment of the evidence which is one of the greatest defects in the professedly *scientific* and *objective* method of the critics. It proves that it is neither objective nor scientific, but on the contrary decidedly subjective and arbitrary.

[37] Eiselen (*Prophetical Books of the O. T.,* Vol. 1, p. 183) includes among six reasons favoring this view the presence of " 'Deuteronomic' conceptions and phrases." This would indicate that this account was subjected to editorial revision as late as the time of Josiah's reign (*cir.* 622 B.C.).

later than the reign of Hezekiah (the Assyrian period). The critics are not agreed as to whether all or most of chaps. 4-5 should be treated as exilic or post-exilic, or whether the words "and thou shalt come to Babylon" and some other passages should be eliminated as later glosses in what may then be regarded as a substantially early document.[38] Many of them are of the opinion that the "situation" of these chapters is different from that of what they regard as the genuine portions of the book. So the alternative, as they see it, is either a late gloss in an early prophetic utterance or the entire utterance is late; two quite effective ways of dealing with the predictive element in this prophecy.

Micah 5:2. This prophecy of the Ruler to be born in Bethlehem is of special interest because in the incident recorded in Matt. 2:1-12 it is mentioned as the one to which "all the chief priests and the scribes of the people" referred Herod when he put to them the question of the Magi, "Where is he that is born King of the Jews?" The answer was precise: "in Bethlehem of Judaea"; and it is undeniable that it is this passage in the Book of Micah which they referred to, a prophecy ancient in Herod's time, even if the critics refuse to admit it to be by Micah the Morashtite. This appeal to Micah makes it quite clear that the Jews of our Lord's day believed that the birth of the Messiah in Bethlehem was foretold centuries before His coming (cf. Jn. 7:42). Such being the case it is not surprising to find this passage in Matt. described as "parabolic"[39] or as a "Christian Midrash rather than authentic history"[40] and that the O. T. passage is all but ignored. For such a treatment of it relieves the commentator of the necessity of admitting that the prophecy of Micah 5:2 is a prediction of the event recorded in Matt. 2:1-12.

Jeremiah 25:11-14. According to the context (v. 1) this prophecy of the captivity in Babylon was uttered in the 4th year of Jehoiakim. The captivity which is soon to commence is to last "seventy years." We are told regarding this chapter, "Almost all scholars agree that the present text of Jer. 25 is an expansion

---

[38] John Paterson tells us that as to chaps. 4-5, "there is a variety of opinion, and many scholars would deny these to Micah" (*The Goodly Fellowship*, p. 86). Nowack (*Die Kleine Propheten*), who accepts the general prediction in 3:12 as genuine, regards the mention of Babylon in 4:10 and most of the verses of chap. 4 as later than Micah.

[39] *Westminster Study Edition* (N. T. section, p. 26): "This story may be a parabolic way of saying that Num. 24:17 has been fulfilled."

[40] "Indeed, it is possible that the story of the Magi is, at any rate in part, a Christian Midrash rather than authentic history, though the compiler of the Gospel may not have recognized its true character" (*A New. Com.* by Gore, Goudge and Guillaume, *in loco*).

from its original form by a later writer," also that "The critical verses are 11-14 and 26*b*."[41] Since it is v. 11 which makes mention of the "seventy years," it is quite obvious why this verse should be regarded as "critical" and assigned to "a later writer", who probably wrote after the captivity was ended!

Jer. 31:31-4. The "New Covenant." This prophecy is quoted in Heb. 8:8-12. It is clearly referred to in the words of Jesus, "this cup is the new testament (covenant) in my blood." This clearly represents the words of Jeremiah as predicting and having their fulfilment in the atoning work of Christ and in the Church which He founded upon it. But we note in the critical interpretation a tendency to represent this prophecy as referring to and capable of fulfilment in Jeremiah's own day. Thus we are told: "Here, then, is the New Covenant (31:31-34) which Jeremiah's own consciousness of fellowship with God led him to see as the only true way to right conduct in practice and belief. That which Jeremiah himself through outward trial and inward struggle had proved true was possible for others."[42] If the New Covenant was introduced in Jeremiah's day and the relationship which it involved was perfectly possible of attainment by him and those who followed his precepts and example, the New Testament "fulfilment" is practically denied.

Jer. 50:1-58. This prophecy which speaks so vividly of the coming downfall of Babylon is assigned by critics to "about 540 B.C." (the very end of the Exile!) because it "reflects like Isa. 40. ff. the historical situation just before the Medes overthrew Babylon, and expresses an attitude towards the latter very different from Jeremiah's own fifty years earlier." Consequently, it is to be inferred that "The compiler, or an editor of the Book, has (51:60) erred in attributing this long prophecy to Jeremiah."[43] The warrant for this statement is significant: "All Oracles or Narratives in the Book, which (apart from obvious intrusions) imply that the Exile is well advanced or that the return from Exile has already happened, or which reflect the circumstances of the Later Exile and subsequent periods or the spirit of Israel and the teaching of her prophets and scribes

---

[41] Creelman, *Introduction*, p. 162.

[42] *A New Commentary* ed. by Gore, Goudge, Guillaume, p. 487, cf. p. 506. The writer of the notes on Jeremiah (B. M. Pickering) does not make any reference to the N. T. interpretation of this passage. The writer of the notes on Hebrews (S. C. Gaylord) remarks: "Even in the time of Jeremiah the old covenant was aged and 'nigh unto vanishing away.' But the writer is thinking of his own time as well" (N. T. section, p. 614). For a similar view, cf. A. C. Welch, *Jeremiah*, pp. 229f.

[43] G. A. Smith, *Jeremiah*, p. 20.

in those periods, we may rule out of the material on which we can rely for our knowledge of Jeremiah's life and his teaching."[44] In other words the critic may *rule out* any material which does not fit into his theory regarding prophecy!

Ezekiel 24:1. For many years the Book of Ezekiel was practically immune from the disintegration which book after book of the Old Testament suffered at the hands of the critics. This was largely due to the fact that so many of the prophecies in the book are definitely dated. There are fourteen of these datings (usually the *day* of the *month* of the *year* is given) between the 5th and the 27th years of the captivity of Jehoiachin (592-570 B.C.). But if the heading of Isa. 13 is set aside and ignored, why should the headings in Ezekiel be regarded as trustworthy? So these headings are regarded as questionable and most or all of them are rejected by the more radical critics.[45] It is also stated repeatedly that Ezekiel belonged to the "captivity" and that he dwelt at or near the river Chebar. This gives his prophecies a definitely Babylonian setting. But if these statements are also set aside, it becomes possible to assert that Ezekiel lived in Jerusalem until its capture by Nebuchadnezzar. Thus 8:1-3 declares expressly that Ezekiel was brought to Jerusalem in vision; and 11:24 tells of his being brought back to Chaldea, to them of the captivity. But if the heading and the statements of 8:1-3 are rejected as spurious,[46] it then becomes possible to argue that Ezekiel was at Jerusalem and actually witnessed the scenes he describes in chaps. 8-11. If such a view is taken, and it must be taken if it is seriously held that Ezekiel was in Jerusalem till the fall of the city, then the words of 24:1f. lose practically all of their significance. For, if Ezekiel was in Jerusalem when the siege began, and not in far off Chaldea, he would not need a special revelation to tell him the day on which the siege began. He would be only too conscious of the fact as a matter of personal experience. It is by methods such as these that both the situation and the scope of even the most definite prophecies

---

[44] *Ibid.,* p. 19.

[45] Two of the most radical are G. Hölscher and Wm. A. Irwin. Hölscher does not hesitate to say: "The Ezekiel Book is, in the form in which it lies before us, just as little a work of the prophet whose name it bears as all the Prophetical Books of the Canon, but it is a much edited work (*ein vielschichtiges Redaktionswerk*) in which the visions and the history of the Prophet Ezekiel form only the kernel (*Kern*)" (*Hesekiel,* p. 26 [1924]).

[46] Irwin is suspicious of all the headings. He classifies 8:1 as "certainly wrong" (*The Problem of Ezekiel,* 1943). Having rejected this heading, he argues from 11:14-25 that Ezekiel "is one of a mournful group numbered for exile after the city had at last fallen on that terrible day in 586" (p. 68f.).

can be changed, and a book like Ezekiel reduced to a collection of late and pseudonymous utterances.

Regarding Ezekiel it may be well to note that the complaint made to the prophet by the children of the captivity, i.e., by the men of his own time, his immediate audience was this: "The vision that he seeth is for many days *to come*, and he prophesieth of the times that are far off" (12:27f.). We observe also that in 33:33 the fulfilment of such long-range predictions is made the test of their genuineness: "And when this cometh to pass (lo, it will come) then shall they know that a prophet hath been among them." Strange words and a strange complaint, if the dictum of Davidson as to the function of the prophet is a correct and adequate one!

Daniel 9 contains a prediction which is dated in "the first year of Darius the son of Ahasuerus, of the seed of the Medes" (v. 1) and is stated to have been made to a certain Daniel who "continued even unto the first year of king Cyrus" (1:21). This gives it, according to the Bible, an approximate date of 538 B.C. There has been much discussion as to the fulfilment of the prophecy. According to what may be called the "traditional" interpretation, the "Messiah" referred to in vv. 25f. is the Lord Jesus Christ. So understood the prediction extends to the First Advent and beyond it. The predictive element is thus very conspicuous in this prophecy. But, according to very many of the critics, the "Messiah" or "anointed one" referred to in this prophecy was the high priest Onias III who was murdered about 171 B.C.; and the termination of the Seventy Weeks was about 168 B.C. And this date, 168 B.C., is the date to which many of them assign the Book of Daniel.[47] Thus, by altering both the situation of the prophecy (making it Maccabean) and the fulfilment (denying its Messianic reference), the critics succeed in eliminating the predictive element in this wonderful prophecy with remarkable thoroughness.[48] By cutting off its head and its feet, as it were, they succeed in fitting it to the Procrustean bed of their theory that prophecy is not predictive!

---

[47] E.g., the *Westminster Study Edition,* p. 1257, cf. p. 1236.

[48] S. R. Driver held that the available evidence favored the conclusion "that the Book of Daniel was not written earlier than *c.* 300 B.C." (*Introduction* 1910, p. 509). He added this significant statement, "More than this can scarcely, in the present state of our knowledge, be affirmed *categorically,* except by those who deny the possibility of predictive prophecy." Such a statement as this, coming as it does from one held in high esteem in critical circles, makes it perfectly plain how prominently the question of the Supernatural figures in the setting of the year 168 B.C. as the date of Daniel by the majority of critical scholars.

What is true of Dan. 9 applies also to the other prophecies in this book. The dreams and visions in Chaps. 2, 7, 8, 10-12 are all stated to have been given to *Daniel* or interpreted by him; they are all dated more or less precisely; and in some cases the situation is definitely stated (5:1, 30; 8:2). All of these prophecies extend into the distant future. Thus, few if any critics will deny that the "he goat" of 8:5-8 is Alexander the Great. Consequently if this vision was seen by Daniel, as 8:1 definitely asserts, it and the others mentioned with it are prophecies whose horizon is the distant future. In the case of chap. 4, the fulfilment began "at the end of twelve months" (v. 29), while the doom pronounced on Belshazzar came true "in that night" (5:30). If the statements which make Daniel the recipient of these visions of dreams are true, predictive prophecy, long range prediction, is possible even from the standpoint of the critics who hold the book to be of Maccabean origin. But the late date of course is regarded as carrying with it the disproof that Daniel uttered any of these predictions.

The above examples, to which others might be added were it necessary, make it unmistakably clear that the claim of the critics that prediction figures only very slightly in prophecy can be made good only by the use of such decidedly drastic methods as the following: (1) Reject the *situation* of the prophecy, as defined in its Biblical context, and assign it to a date so near the so-called fulfilment, that the element of prediction is largely or wholly eliminated; (2) Tone down the prophecy either by cutting out or interpreting away its distinctive features so that the prediction becomes vague or general; (3) Treat the predictive element as simply a literary device employed to enable a contemporary or near-contemporary of the events described to speak with the authority of a prophetic voice from the distant past; (4) Insist that, in the case of all the prophetical books, "later editorial hands undoubtedly labored on the prophecies and brought the book to its present form,"[49] a claim which, if admitted, makes it quite uncertain what the prophet said, and what the successive revisers and editors of his utterances have made him say. It is only when the voice of prophecy has been silenced or muffled by the application of such methods as these that the desired result can be obtained. Prophecy then ceases to be predictive, because it ceases to be prophecy according to the *Bible* and has become prophecy according to the *Critics*.

Only those who are unfamiliar with the statements of the Bible itself will be impressed by the oft-repeated claim of the critics that their theory regarding prophecy is based on a careful, objective, and scientific study of the Biblical data. When the Biblical witnesses are allowed to testify and their testimony, as recorded in the Bible, is accepted as trustworthy, the result is very different. It is in fact a complete *exposé* of the falsity of the claims of the critics.

EMPHASIS ON ORIGINAL MEANING

Closely related to the two outstanding features in the critical interpretation of Prophecy—situation and scope—which have just been considered, is the emphasis which is placed on the importance and even the necessity of determining the *original* meaning of a prophetic utterance, what it meant to the one who uttered it, what meaning it had for those who were the first to hear it; and to distinguish this primary meaning from the meaning which it has for later generations or acquires in the light of its fulfilment. Thus we are told: "Our first question must necessarily be: 'What meaning did the human author intend to be attached to his words?' and it is not until this question has been fairly faced and answered, that we can legitimately proceed to inquire what further significance may be attached to the words as forming part of the one great continuous revelation of God by the Spirit dividing to every man severally as He will."[50] This subject will be dealt with more fully in the next chapter. In this connection it will suffice to point out that it tends to draw a distinction, which may easily be developed into a radical difference, between what the prophet, as a man of his own time, speaking to the people of his own time, meant by his words and the meaning which later generations living under quite different conditions may have rightly or wrongly attached to them. When the prophet is viewed primarily as one who interprets the events of his own time to his *contemporaries,* the only "fulfilment" which future generations can find in his words for their day must consist in the bearing of the principles which he enunciated and of his estimate of the events through which he was passing on the changed conditions of a future far too remote for him to foresee it or to deal directly with its circumstances and its events. But so understood the prophet is practically transformed into a moral philosopher, whose predictions become little more than maxims which are applicable *mutatis mutandis* to every succeeding age.

---

[50] Edgehill, *An Enquiry into the Evidential Value of Prophecy,* p. 33. Cf. A. C. Zenos, art. "Prophecy" in *A New Standard Bible Dictionary,* p. 742.

CHAPTER II

PROPHECY ACCORDING TO THE BIBLE

To determine what is the Biblical conception of prophecy, we cannot do better than to turn to that passage in Deuteronomy (18:9-22) which speaks of the Prophet who is to come. The situation of this utterance is practically the same as that of chap. 28 which has been referred to above. Moses is speaking to the children of Israel, encamped in the land of Moab just before his death. The reference of the utterance is quite definitely to the future: "when thou art come into the land." Moses first warns his hearers against the "abominations" by means of which the inhabitants of the land which Israel is to possess have endeavored to know and if possible to control the future. Nine different methods used by them are enumerated. We do not know the exact nature of some of these practices nor the precise differences between them all. But the length of the list serves to stress a fact which both the Classics of Greece and Rome and, more recently, the spade of the archaeologist have made almost appallingly clear, how powerful and how dire was the spell which the thought of the unknown and yet inevitable future cast over the living and thinking of the men of the long ago. Ezekiel tells us in a vivid picture, how the king of Assyria used three different forms of divination (21:21) to determine the direction he should take when setting out on one of his many campaigns. No one of these is expressly mentioned here. But one of the three, "he looked into the liver," refers to a rite *(hepatoscopy)* which was very extensively used. A large number of omen texts dealing with this subject have been discovered. We might almost call it a science, irrational and absurd as it seems to us to be.[1]

This impressive introduction to the prophecy illustrates the tremendous role which the problem of the future played in the ancient world in general and particularly among the peoples

---

[1] Cf. Isa. 47:9-13 and Jer. 27:9 which mention several of these practices. A striking illustration of the tremendous hold which such rites had over the men and women of antiquity is given in Vergil's description of the frenzied efforts of lovesick Dido to penetrate by means of divination the hidden future and to win the favor of the gods (*Aeneid* iv. 60-64). It may be freely rendered as follows:
"Dido, so lovely herself, in her right hand holding the chalice,
Pours out between the horns of the snow-white heifer libation.
Or she goes to the shrines of the gods, to altars of fatlings.
There she ceaselessly offers her gifts and breathlessly peering
Into their yawning breasts, she questions the quivering entrails."

whose land Israel was to possess. It also prepares most effectively for the disclosure of that better means of dealing with this vastly important and intriguing problem, which God is providing for His people. All the abominations of the heathen are to be rejected as worthless and evil, because "The LORD thy God will raise up unto thee a prophet from the midst of thee, of thy brethren, like unto me; unto him ye shall hearken."[2] With these words Moses describes briefly the nature of Biblical prophecy. The Lord will "raise up" the prophet, the prophet will be an Israelite, he will enjoy a position of intimacy with God and of authority with men such as only Moses has enjoyed (Nu. 7:89; 12:8).

It is important to observe that Moses takes occasion at this point to call attention to a significant and remarkable fact,—that the disclosure of the divine purpose which he is now making to Israel had already been made to him personally nearly forty years before at Sinai, when the people after hearing the proclamation of the Ten Commandments by the voice of God Himself, requested that they might not again hear God speaking directly to them lest they die (Ex. 20:19). No hint of this great revelation is given in the account of the majestic scene at Sinai. It was made known to Moses. But Israel did not need it so long as Moses was with them. Consequently, this prophecy may be said to have two *situations:* the situation at Sinai when the Lord revealed it to Moses, the situation in the land of Moab when Moses declared it to the people.

Having briefly explained the original occasion of the revelation which he now makes known to the people, Moses repeats and elaborates it. He begins with a word of commendation: "And the LORD said unto me, They have well spoken that which they have spoken." Such a spectacle as Israel had witnessed at Sinai was too awful, too appalling, to be the usual and customary method of making known the will of God to His people. So the Lord declares, "I will raise them up a prophet from among their brethren, like unto thee"; and He adds these words which express so clearly the function of the prophet: "and I will put my words in his mouth: and he shall speak unto them all that I shall command him." This is the office of the prophet. He is a spokesman for God. And because he is a "man of God," who

---

[2] This is apparently the meaning of Num. 23:23, of which the best rendering seems to be: "For there is no divination in Jacob and no sorcery in Israel. According to the time [i.e., at the proper time, or, from time to time] it will be told to Israel and to Jacob what God is going to do [or "has done" in the sense of the prophetic perfect "will do"].

speaks the "word of God," the Lord Himself will "require it" of the man who does not hearken to the voice of His messenger.

It is made quite clear in the New Testament that this prophecy regarding the prophet has had its full and final fulfilment in the Messiah (Acts 3:22; 7:37 cf. Jn. 1:21; 6:14; 7:40). But it is hardly less clear that it must also have reference in a lesser degree to that long line of prophetic men who came after Moses and were like Moses in this regard, that the Lord raised them up from among their brethren, put His word into their mouths, and commissioned them to declare unto His people all that He commanded them. The test of true prophecy given in vv. 20-24 makes this sufficiently clear. For if prophecy were to be restricted to the One Prophet of the future, it would have no reference at all to that most significant movement which was to figure for more than half a millennium so prominently in Israel's history—"the goodly fellowship of the prophets." It is significant that Peter, in appealing to the Old Testament in his sermon in Solomon's porch, directly connects Moses' prediction concerning the Prophet with the course of O.T. prophecy in general by adding the words: "Yea, and all the prophets from Samuel and those that follow after, as many as have spoken, have likewise foretold of these days" (Acts 3:22-24).

On the other hand it is to be observed that while the words "like unto thee" have an application to and fulfilment in every prophet whom the Lord raised up to be His spokesman to His people, there is nevertheless an important difference in the mode of communication which is not to be overlooked. This is stated very definitely in Num. 12:1-8, where the difference between Moses and the prophets is made very clear. In the case of the ordinary prophet, so the Lord declares, "I will make myself known unto him in a vision, *and* will speak unto him in a dream."[3] This mode of revelation is contrasted with the "mouth to mouth" communion which Moses enjoyed (7:89, cf. Deut. 34:10) and which was only fully realized in the perfect communion which Jesus had with the Father. A contrast is also drawn here between "apparently" or "manifestly" and "in dark speeches," which implies that there will be or may be an element

---

[3] Elsewhere "dream" is hardly ever used of revelations received by the prophets (cf. Dan. 7:1). Dreams were given to Jacob, Joseph, Solomon, and doubtless to many others, also to Pharaoh and Nebuchadnezzar. It is also used of the "dreams" of the false prophets (Jer. 23:25-32). Several Hebrew words are rendered by "vision" in AV and RV. There seems to be little difference between them. The word used here (*mar'ah*) is found chiefly in Ezek. and Dan. The most frequently occurring word (*chazon*) is used in Isa. 1 and also in Ezek. and Dan.

of obscurity in the utterances of the prophets; and this we often find to be the case.[4] It is to be noted further that the word "vision" is used of the prophecies of a number of the prophets, though it is more usual to speak of the "word," which the prophet declared from the Lord. *Seeing* and *hearing* were the two means by which the Lord communicated His will to the prophets. How close was the relationship between them is illustrated by the expression, "this is the word which the Lord hath shewed me (literally, caused me to see)" (Jer. 38:21).

What then is the Biblical conception of the function of the prophet? It is simply this, to declare to men the "word" which God places "in his mouth." He is a spokesman for God; and the only limitation placed upon his words is that they must be *God's* words.[5] It is because of this that we constantly find the prophets introducing their messages by such impressive phrases as: "Thus saith the Lord," "The word of the Lord came unto me saying." It is the false prophets who speak words "out of their own heart" (Ezek. 13:2, 17). The true prophet is a "man of God" and it is his sole duty to declare the "word" of God, as God has revealed it to him, the "vision" which God has caused him to see.

The Situation of the Prophecies

In view of the insistence of the critics on the importance, even the necessity, of determining the situation of every prophecy if its meaning and significance is to be properly understood, it is important to consider carefully the way in which this matter is dealt with in the Bible itself. If we turn to the Biblical record, and especially to the examples of predictive prophecy which were discussed in Chapter I., we observe such facts as the following:

(1) The prophecy may be *dated*. This dating may be precise: "in the fortieth year, in the eleventh month, on the first day of the month" (Deut. 1:3), "in the fourth year of Jehoiakim the son of Josiah king of Judah, which was the first year of Nebu-

---

[4] Regarding the reticence and indefiniteness which often characterizes prophecy, Principal Fairbairn has well said: "And in nothing, perhaps, more than in this wonderful combination of darkness and light observable in the prophetic word—in the clear foreknowledge it displays, on the one hand, of the greater things to come in Providence, coupled, on the other, with only such indications of time and place as might be sufficient to stimulate inquiry, and ultimately dispel doubt, may we discern the directing agency of Him who knows our frame, and knows as well what is fit to be withheld as what to be imparted in supernatural communications" (*Prophecy*, 2nd Eng. ed., pp. 180f.).
[5] The basic test of all prophecy is stated clearly in Deut. 13:1-5, cf. Isa. 8:19f. The law of God as contained in essence in the Decalogue is the test of every "Thus saith the Lord."

chadnezzar king of Babylon" (Jer. 25:1), "in the five and twentieth year of our captivity, in the beginning of the year, in the tenth day of the month, in the fourteenth year after the city was smitten" (Ezek. 40:1). It may also be more or less indefinite or refer to events the date of which is now unknown: "in the days of Ahaz, the son of Jotham, king of Judah" (Isa. 7:1), "in the year that Tartan came unto Ashdod" (20:1), Merodach-baladan's embassy, "for he had heard that he had been sick, and was recovered" (39:1), "two years before the earthquake" (Amos 1:1, cf. Zech. 14:5).

(2) The *situation* or *occasion* may be made clear in various ways: Jacob is on his death bed (Gen. 49:1, 33), Israel is on the border of Moab (Num. 22:1), Hannah is rejoicing in giving Samuel to the Lord (1 Sam. 1:24-2:1), Saul's disobedience (1 Sam. 13:13f.), David's desire to build a house for the Lord (2 Sam. 7:1), Solomon's apostasy in his old age (1 Kgs. 11:11), Jeroboam's dedication (?) of the altar at Bethel (1 Kgs. 13:1), Ahab in Naboth's garden (1 Kgs. 21:18f.), Jehu's well-doing (2 Kgs. 10:30). Such passages as these suffice to show that according to the Bible itself many of the prophecies which it records had very definite situations and occasions; and we are often told more or less fully just what these occasions were. And it is especially to be noted that all of these situations indicate quite clearly that the prophecy which was then uttered was a prediction, that it concerned the future. Thus, we do not know just when the Naboth incident occurred, how long before Ahab's defeat and death. But we are told that Elijah's prediction of the downfall of his house and the awful end of Jezebel, a prediction which was not completely fulfilled for more than a decade after his death, was made to him by Elijah face to face.

(3) The *name* of the prophet may simply be given. In the case of such headings as "The vision of Obadiah," "The burden which Habakkuk the prophet did see," "The word of the LORD that came to Joel the son of Pethuel," we may assume that these men were well-known in their day, and that the mere mention of the name was sufficient to date their messages at least approximately. In such cases further information is given either in the book itself or elsewhere in Scripture. Thus, Habakkuk prophesied concerning the Chaldeans, Jonah lived in the time of Jeroboam II (2 Kgs. 14:25). Joel's position as the second of the Minor Prophets indicates an early date, although most critics favor a late one.

(4) The *period* during which the prophet lived and labored may be indicated. This is the case with Isaiah, Jeremiah, Hosea,

Micah, Zephaniah. In the case of these prophecies it has been customary to regard the heading as applying to the entire contents of the book at the head of which each is placed. It is only when these headings are ignored and the books are cut apart and the fragments regarded as independent or isolated utterances, that the claim of the critics that *anonymity* is characteristic of many or most of the prophetical utterances of the Old Testament becomes an "assured result" of the Higher Criticism.[6] Isaiah, for example, only becomes a "little library" of prophecies, mostly anonymous, when the general heading is ignored and the book is split up into a hundred or more fragments, for each of which a "situation" must be found quite regardless of the general situation given in 1:1.

It is clear, then, that the Bible does attach importance to the authorship, date, and situation of the prophetic utterances which it records; and it attaches importance to them mainly, it would seem, for a reason which is quite obvious, because they are or may be *predictions*.

The Scope of the Prophecies

The reader has of course noted that all of the examples of prophecy considered in Chapter I. were selected and discussed as examples of *predictive* prophecy. It is the predictive element which often makes the Biblical situation so important. For according to their Biblical situation these predictions reveal an insight into the future which clearly transcends anything that is possible to the dim and short-sighted vision of mortal man. As in the case of these prophecies the situation and authorship are sometimes defined more precisely than in others, but usually with sufficient definiteness to make it clear that they are predictive, so the *scope* of these prophecies may and does vary considerably. It may be "three-score and five years" (Isa. 7:8), "seventy years" (23:15; Jer. 25:11), "four generations" (2 Kgs. 10:30), "four hundred years" (Gen. 15:13). It may be quite short: "three years" (Isa. 16:14; cf. 20:3), "within a year"

---

[6] Each of the books comprising the Latter Prophets (Isaiah to Malachi), even the smallest of them (Obadiah) bears at least the name of an individual as its author. About a score of other prophets are mentioned by name in the other books of the Old Testament, e.g., Ahijah, Elijah, Nathan, Shemaiah. Anonymity is exceptional in the case of a prophet whose words are recorded (e.g., 1 Kgs. 13:1). It is quite true that we know relatively little about most of these prophets, only the little that the Bible tells us. But that does not make them anonymous. We do not know whether the Sosthenes of 1 Cor. 1:1 is the same person as the chief ruler of the synagogue mentioned in Acts 18:17. But Paul and the Christians at Corinth undoubtedly knew; and we cannot justly hold them responsible for our ignorance.

(21:16), "tomorrow" (2 Kgs. 7:1). It may be less definite as to time, yet precise as to the event (1 Kgs. 13:1f.). It may have its fulfilment in a definite event or series of events (Isa. 13:1, cf. v. 17) or it may state a principle of the divine government which may have several or many fulfilments (Deut. 28). It may also, and this is the great burden of prophecy, refer to the Messianic age and have its fulfilment in it, as the New Testament frequently asserts that it has done (Isa. 7:14, cf. Matt. 1:22f.; Mic. 5:2, cf. Matt. 2:5f.; Ps. 110:1, cf. Matt. 22:41-46).

It is quite evident (Deut. 18:9-14), that one reason for the powerful appeal which the religions of their neighbors made upon the Israelites is to be found in this very fact, that they claimed to be able to satisfy this craving for knowledge of coming events which is so natural to man as he faces the unknown but inevitable future. Consequently, appeal to heathen gods or the use of divination is treated as an affront to the God of Israel which He will "require" of the guilty (Dt. 18:19). Ahaziah of Israel was ill and naturally desired to know whether his case was hopeful or not. So he sent to inquire of Baal-zebub the god of Ekron (2 Kgs. 1:2). This provoked Elijah's indignant and wrathful words: "Is it because there is no God in Israel, that ye go to inquire of Baal-zebub the god of Ekron?" This stated the issue definitely and sharply. Elijah stigmatized Ahaziah's act as treason and apostasy. The final act of disobedience which marked the tragic career of Saul was that when the Lord answered him neither "by dreams, by Urim, or by prophets" (1 Sam. 28:6), all of them proper and legitimate ways of ascertaining the future, he resorted to a woman with a familiar spirit to learn the result of the coming battle with the Philistines (1 Chr. 10:13f.). Isaiah answers the suggestion that the men of his day resort to these unlawful means of learning the future with the words: "Should not a people seek unto their God? for the living *should they seek* unto the dead?" (Isa. 8:19). And we should not forget that this desire to know the future, which was so keenly felt in ancient times, is just as strong today. Astrology, palmistry, crystal-gazing, ouija boards, spiritualism and its seances, have a strange fascination for multitudes of so-called modern-minded people. Where true Christian faith is feeble or wholly absent, superstitions, even the most absurd, tend to appear and to flourish. To endeavor, therefore, to minimize the importance of the element of prediction or to eliminate it from the prophecies of the Bible as the critics are constantly endeavoring to do is to seek to get rid of those very things which respond to the deepest longings of mankind and to turn them back to those false and abominable ways which are so strongly denounced in the Bible, which points out so plainly the other and better way.

THE VIEWPOINT OF THE PROPHET

As soon as it is recognized that the future figured prominently in the utterances of the prophets, it becomes important to observe carefully the different ways in which these coming events are spoken of by them. Sometimes they referred to them quite definitely as future events. We have already noted that such expressions as "behold the days are coming" are frequently used by them. But it is easy to understand that men who like the prophets were constantly thinking in terms of the future and regarded the visions of coming events which they received from God as certain of fulfilment because revealed to them by God Himself, might at times become so absorbed in the future and so engrossed with its events and see them so vividly presented to their spiritual sight as to speak of these future events as if they were living among them and these things were actually transpiring before their eyes. The very vividness of such visions of the future would make this both natural and likely. A striking example is Jer. 4:23-26: "I beheld the earth, and, lo, it was without form, and void; and the heavens and they *had* no light. I beheld the mountains, and, lo, they trembled, and all the hills moved lightly. I beheld, and, lo, there was no man, and all the birds of the heavens were fled. I beheld, and, lo, the fruitful field *was* a wilderness, and all the cities thereof were broken down at the presence of the LORD, *and* by his fierce anger." The prophet is describing what he has seen. Four times the ominous "I beheld" is repeated. He has seen with his own eyes a devastation so terrible that he describes it in terms which suggest a return to primitive chaos. Yet he goes on at once to say: "For thus saith the LORD, The whole land shall be a desolation; yet will I not make a full end." Whether this cataclysm is imminent and at the hands of the Scythians, or whether the prophet is speaking of a far greater overthrow of which the Scythian peril is but a type, he does not tell us. To what extent it may be eschatological, we do not know. The important point is that the prophet has seen a vision of this terrible calamity and describes it as if it had already taken place; while at the same time declaring that he is speaking of the future, of things to come. To this vivid way of describing future events is due a feature of the Biblical style which is called the *Prophetic Perfect*.

THE PROPHETIC PERFECT

In Hebrew the perfect tense is ordinarily used to describe past events or actions. Such events are "perfect," because completed (perfected) in the past or at the time of speaking. But we often find in the language of prophecy that the perfect tense is used to describe events which lie in the future. This is the case because, from the standpoint of the purpose of God of which they are the declaration, their occurrence is to be regarded as so certain that they can be spoken of as "perfect," as if they had already taken place. S. R. Driver, a leading critical scholar in his day, has described this "as the most special and remarkable use of the tense." He says of it, ". . . its abrupt appearance in this capacity imparts to descriptions of the future a forcible and expressive touch of reality, and reproduces vividly the certainty with which the occurrence of a yet future event is contemplated by the speaker. Sometimes the perfect appears thus only for a single word; sometimes, as though nothing more than an ordinary series of past historical events were being described, it extends over many verses in succession: continually the series of perfects is interspersed with the simple future forms, as the prophet shifts his point of view, at one moment contemplating the events he is describing from the *real standpoint* of the present, at another moment looking back upon them as accomplished and done, and so viewing them from an *ideal position* in the future."[7] In view of the claim so insistently made by the critics, among whom Driver held high rank, that the position or situation of the prophet must always be actual and real, that he cannot speak from the viewpoint of a future and "non-existent situation," the above statement is worthy of very careful pondering. For it amounts to a very definite admission that the language of prophecy differs from that of history in this very respect, that the prophet may and often does speak from the standpoint of the future and in so doing describes things future as though they were already past.

The occurrence of this *prophetic perfect* is somewhat obscured for the English reader by the fact that it is sometimes rendered in the English versions by the present or future tense. Thus, in Num. 24:17 "a star has come out of Jacob" is the correct rendering. But since the perfect is followed by futures, both AV and ARV render it by the future, "there shall come (forth) a Star." Isa. 5:13 begins with the perfect, "therefore my people have gone into captivity." But in v. 14 the natural rendering is "shall descend"; and many scholars regard the captivity referred to as still future. Isa. 9:1ff. has a series of perfects: "has seen . . . light has shined upon them . . . they rejoiced . . . thou hast

---

[7] *Hebrew Tenses* (3rd ed.), pp. 18f. Most of the examples which follow will be found in Driver.

broken . . : a child has been born . . . a son has been given . . .
and his name has been called . . ." Yet the events described are
clearly future. Regarding the vivid picture of the advance of
the Assyrian given in Isa. 10:28-32, Duhm, one of the radical
critics of Isaiah, has said: "Despite the perfects it deals not
with a past but a future occurrence." In Isa. 24:4-12 the perfect
tense is used nearly always (24 out of 28 times). Note especially "the city of confusion has been broken down" (v. 10).[8]
In 28:2 "has cast down" (AV, "shall") represents the destruction of Samaria as already taken place. But the perfect is followed by the future, "shall be trodden under foot." We find exactly the same thing in the Second Part of Isaiah. In 43:14 we
read "For your sake I have sent to Babylon, and have brought
down all their nobles . . ." In Isa. 45:17 we are told "Israel has
been saved in the LORD with an everlasting salvation"; and in
46:1f. the humiliation of the gods of Babylon is pictured as
already taken place, "Bel has bowed down . . . they themselves
have gone into captivity." Similarly in 48:20 the exiles are commanded to go forth from Babylon and to proclaim these glorious
tidings to the ends of the earth (land): "The LORD hath redeemed his servant Jacob." Yet according to the critical viewpoint, the prophet regards the fall of Babylon as still future
though very near at hand![9]

Jeremiah's prophecy of the downfall of Babylon (chaps. 50-51)
is cast in a similar mould. It begins with a burst of triumph,
"Declare ye among the nations, and publish, and set up a
standard; publish *and* conceal not: say, Babylon is taken, Bel
is confounded, Merodach is broken in pieces; her idols are
confounded, her images are broken in pieces." And the reason
is given: "For out of the north there has come up (not, "cometh
up," A.V.) a nation against her." Compare, "How is the hammer

---

[8] With what lively and confident expectancy the prophet looks forward to the
time of blessing which is to follow the chastening is illustrated by Isa. 14:4f.
and 26:1-6 where he even puts on the lips of those who will live in those
glorious future days a "proverb" or taunt song, or a song of thanksgiving and
praise which will be suited to the occasion. According to G. L. Robinson, "The
prophet's fundamental standpoint in chs. 24-27 is the same as that of 2:2-4 and
13:23. Yet the prophet not infrequently throws himself forward into the remote
future, oscillating backward and forward between his own times and those of
Israel's restoration. It is especially noteworthy how he sustains himself in a
long and continued transportation of himself to the period of Israel's redemption" (Article "Isaiah" in *Intern. Stand. Bible Encyc.*, p. 1499).

[9] In *Isaiah, His Life and Times* (1888), Driver argues that the transference
to the future is only "momentary" and furnishes no analogy for such "sustained
transference to the future as would be implied if these chapters were by Isaiah"
(pp. 186f.). G. A. Smith, *The Book of Isaiah* (vol. ii., p. 9) takes the same attitude. This means that the validity of the principle is to be admitted but its
application to Isa. 40-66 is to be denied.

of the whole earth cut asunder and broken! How is Babylon become a desolation among the nations!" (v. 23), "Babylon is suddenly fallen and destroyed; howl for her" (51:8), "How is Sheshach taken" (vv. 41f.), cf. vv. 55, 56. Here we have a striking intermingling of prophetic past, present, and future, which gives the description remarkable vividness. The method of presentation obviously resembles Isa. 40-48 to a remarkable degree. Yet it is definitely stated in 51:64, "Thus far *are* the words of Jeremiah." And Jeremiah probably died in Egypt before the death of Nebuchadnezzar whose invasion of Egypt in 568 B.C. twenty years after the fall of Jerusalem was definitely foretold by the prophet (43:8-13).

The use of the Prophetic Perfect is very striking in certain of the Psalms. The 2nd Psalm describes a revolt of the "kings of earth," which is actually taking place. "Why have the nations raged?" It is a raging already begun and still continuing. "Why do they rage?" Their counsels are vividly described: "Let us break their bands asunder, and cast away their cords from us." It is all in vain. For the Lord declares: "I have set my king upon my holy hill of Zion." The king declares the contents of the decree: "Thou art my Son. This day [today] have I begotten thee." And in view of the irresistible might promised to Him, the rebels are exhorted to submission, prompt and abject: "Be wise now therefore O ye kings . . . Kiss the Son, lest he be angry." Clearly the writer is describing these events as one who is living in the midst of them. Yet this language describes a world-wide revolt; and there is no psalm in the entire Psalter which is quoted more frequently than this one, or referred more definitely for its fulfilment to New Testament times. Its "today," so Paul tells us, was fulfilled in the resurrection of Christ (Acts 13:33, cf. Rom. 1:4). The same applies to the 110th Psalm. The imperatives "sit . . . rule" make the situation as vividly present as is the case in Ps. 2. Yet in vv. 5f. we read twice "has smitten . . . has smitten." Consequently, we are told, according to the critical interpretation, "The point which is usually emphasized most strongly is that a contemporary king is addressed, not a future king foretold."[10] Yet this psalm is treated in the New Testament as both Davidic and Messianic. Ps. 22 uses the Prophetic Perfect repeatedly to describe the sufferings of the Afflicted. In this respect it closely resembles Isaiah 53, as we shall see presently. To what extent it describes the actual sufferings of the Psalmist, David, according to the heading, we

---

[10] Baethgen, *Die Psalmen*, p. 336.

cannot say. But that it had a fuller and a Messianic import is made quite clear in the New Testament (Matt. 27:35).[11]

The above examples make it clear that there is a marked tendency for the language of prophecy to refer to future events, even events lying in a distant future, as already past. Sometimes the change back to the use of the future tense is made very soon. Sometimes the perfect is used more or less consistently throughout the entire description. If this is admitted—it is hard to see how it can be denied—the only question of importance is as to the extent to which the prophet can maintain this ideal viewpoint; and this can only be determined by a careful induction based on all the relevant passages. For the moment, it is sufficient to observe that the data we have just been examining make it quite obvious that the sweeping assertion that the prophet must always speak from the standpoint of his own time and that the situation of a prophecy can only be determined by the events and circumstances which it describes and the way in which it describes them, must be very greatly modified, if it is to be brought into harmony with the evidence that the language of prophecy may and does differ quite appreciably from that of history in this very respect, that it can speak of future events as if they had already taken place.

THE ORIGINAL MEANING OF PROPHECY

In view of the emphasis placed by the critics upon the *original meaning* of the words of the Prophets, by which is meant, the meaning which his words had for the prophet himself and the meaning which he intended his hearers to draw from them, it is important to examine carefully the attitude of the Bible as a whole to this question. When we do so, we discover that ordinarily the Bible makes no distinction between what the prophet said and what he meant. Rather it allows and expects us to infer *his* meaning and *the* meaning of his words from what he actually said. Thus we read that Elisha said to the king's favorite, who openly challenged the prophet's promise of plenty for the starving people of Samaria, "Behold, thou shalt see it with thine eyes, but shalt not eat thereof" (2 Kgs. 7:2). We are left completely in the dark as to exactly what his words meant to Elisha himself, to the king, to his favorite, or to the people who heard them. Did Elisha realize that he was predicting the death of the king's favorite? Did the king realize that he was placing his favorite in a position which would lead to his destruction,

---

[11] A. F. Kirkpatrick, The *Psalms*, p. 114.

or did he perhaps think that he was placing him in a position of honor which would make the threat of the prophet meaningless or ineffectual? Did the people who trod on the favorite in the gate realize that they were fulfilling the prophecy to the letter? We cannot answer one of these interesting and intriguing questions with certainty. Yet here we have a prediction which fulfils every condition laid down by Davidson. The prophet is dealing with an actual present situation. He is speaking as a man of his own time to the men of his own time and of a matter which is of great importance to them. And the death of the favorite even more than the unexpected plenty at which he scoffed, was the signal proof that what Elisha foretold was "the word of the LORD." Yet we cannot even be sure that the death of the favorite was any less of a surprise to Elisha than it clearly must have been to the king.

We may ask the same questions regarding the Prayer of Hannah, which we have already discussed in a different connection. Hannah's concluding words are these: "The LORD shall judge the ends of the earth; and he shall give strength unto his king, and exalt the horn of his anointed." The Bible tells us plainly and definitely that Hannah uttered these words. It does not tell us what she meant by them, or what she understood them to mean. It does not tell us who heard her utter them, or who recorded them. It does not tell us whether she lived to see her son anoint Saul to be king of Israel, or whether she learned of the anointing of David. We may hesitate to say that she realized the full meaning of her words. There is not entire unanimity even today among scholars as to their full import. What we are told is simply that she uttered them. Consequently, when the critics tell us that such an utterance is quite out of keeping with Hannah's situation and spiritual insight and must date from a far later period, they are denying what the Bible expressly affirms; and they are presuming to know far more about Hannah and her circumstances than can possibly be the case.

In Jer. 3:16 we read these amazing words: "And it shall come to pass, when ye be multiplied and increased in the land, in those days, saith the LORD, they shall no more say, The ark of the covenant of the LORD: neither shall it come to mind: neither shall they remember it; neither shall they visit it; neither shall that be done any more." This is one of the most remarkable prophecies in the whole Old Testament. What did Jeremiah mean by it? Did he foresee that the ark would not return from Babylon, at the close of the seventy-year captivity which he was

later to foretell, that unlike the golden candlestick, it would not
be among the 5400 vessels of gold and silver which Sheshbazzar
would bring up from Babylon to Jerusalem? Did he realize that
he was speaking of that far distant time, of which our Lord spake
to the woman at the well, when all over the world the true
worshippers would worship the Father in spirit and in truth (Jn.
4:23)? If so, how did he reconcile such a prediction with the
one recorded in 17:19-27 where temple worship at Jerusalem
in future days is described in some detail? The only hint which
is given us as to what Jeremiah understood by his words is in
the further declaration of 3:17 that all Jerusalem shall be called
"the throne of the Lord," which means apparently that the holy
city shall become a vast holy of holies where the Lord shall dwell
in the midst of a holy people even as He had dwelt, or sat
enthroned above the ark and between the cherubim, in the holy
of holies of the tabernacle and the temple (Zech. 14:20f). But
just how much of the meaning and implications of this tremendous utterance the prophet himself appreciated and understood it is impossible for us to determine with any degree of
accuracy.

There are at least three things which must be considered as
bearing on this question as to the meaning which the prophet
himself attached to the prophetic word which was revealed to
him.

(1) The Bible as a rule is very reticent as to the feelings and
ideas and opinions which the recipients of divine truth enter-
tained with regard to it. The account of the command given to
Abraham to sacrifice his son and of Abraham's obedience is
amazingly brief. As to the command itself we are told only
that it was given to "test" Abraham. What Abraham thought of
this command, the agony of mind which it caused him, how far
he undertood its purpose, and how far he succeeded in recon-
ciling it with the promise which had been made to him and
which centred in Isaac—of this the Genesis account tells us
almost nothing. The command, the obedience, and the consequences of the obedience are allowed to speak for themselves.
In Ezek. 24 the death of the prophet's wife is foretold and we
read, "So I spake unto the people in the morning: and at even
my wife died; and I did in the morning as I was commanded."
Then we read the reason for the singular command given to
the prophet. The event is recorded so briefly and so objectively,
that some commentators hold that we are dealing here not with
an actual occurrence but with a parable or vision. Whether such
is the case or not, the important fact is that the prophet was told

to do something and he did it. How he felt about it and how fully he appreciated its significance is a secondary matter.

(2) It is also to be remembered that the New Testament tells us quite plainly that the Old Testament prophets did not at times fully understand the meaning of the words which they uttered. They "inquired and sought diligently" the meaning of the things which the Spirit of Christ which was in them did signify; and it was made plain to them that in-speaking of these things they were ministering to generations yet unborn (1 Pet. 1:10f.). In the first chapter of Hebrews, for example, the writer forms a catena of passages from the Old Testament to show the utter uniqueness of the Son of God. How fully the writers of the Old Testament passages appreciated their Messianic significance and implications may not be clear to us. But the inspired New Testament writer finds it there, and gives us the New Testament meaning of Old Testament Scripture. And it is this New Testament significance which is especially important to the New Testament Christian.[12]

(3) The New Testament also makes it clear that the Old Testament prophets and inspired writers sometimes at least knew far more of the meaning and implication of their words than we would otherwise suppose to be the case. One of the most signal illustrations of this is given us in Peter's Speech on the day of Pentecost. In this great address which is made up so largely of quotations from the Old Testament Peter tells us for example regarding the 16th Psalm not only that its closing words have their fulfilment in the resurrection of Christ, but that David who uttered them, *being a prophet* and "seeing this before spake of the resurrection of Christ, that his soul was not left in hell, neither his flesh did see corruption" (Acts 2:31). In other words David was not speaking of his own resurrection, but of that of the great Scion of his house in Whom alone the endless duration promised to his kingship could be realized (2 Sam. 7:13, 16, 24, 25, 29). Yet according to most if not all of the critics, such a belief would have been an utter anachronism in the case of David, an idea quite incompatible with their entire theory of the development in Israel of the doctrine of life after death and of resurrection. In view of this fact we need to remember that Jesus said to the Jews, "Your father Abraham rejoiced to see my day: and he saw it and was glad"

---

[12] The matter has been well stated by B. B. Warfield, "What Jesus and the writers of the New Testament saw in the Messianic references of the Psalms, it is natural that those who share their viewpoint should also see in them" ("The Divine Messiah in the Old Testament," *Princeton Theol. Rev.*, vol. xiv, p. 373).

(Jn. 8:56). These are wonderfully suggestive words; and we get some idea of their meaning when we study the comment on Gen. 22 which is given us in Heb. 11. It has been charged that Abraham simply lied when he said to his servants: "Abide ye here with the ass: and I and the lad will go yonder and worship and come again to you" (v. 5). But in Hebrews the real state of Abraham's mind is described in the words: "accounting that God was able to raise him up even from the dead; from whence also he received him in a figure" (11:19). This inspired interpretation gives us an amazing insight into the mind of Abraham; and it shows us that Abraham's sublime obedience was the result of a sublime faith, which made the obedience possible and to us understandable. Such an example as this should make the Bible student hesitate to assert too positively or definitely just what the Old Testament prophets must have meant or cannot have meant by their words or what they understood them to mean.

If we take Abraham as an example and study his life carefully, we will conclude that Abraham was a man of his own time who accepted its standards and even failed to live up to them (Gen. 20:9), and *also* that Abraham was a man who was far ahead of his time and that the revelations which were made to him are still marching on to their fulfilment. The words, "in thy seed shall all the nations of the earth be blessed," may have meant much or little to Abraham. They were, we know, like a closed book to generations of his descendants; and when his great descendant Paul the Apostle to the Gentiles spoke of the time of their fulfilment as already arrived by quoting the words of the command given him by the risen and ascended Christ, "Depart: for I will send thee far hence unto the Gentiles," his brethren of the seed of Abraham lifted up their voices and said, "Away with such a fellow from the earth: for it is not fit that he should live" (Acts 22:22). The question is not what these wonderful words meant to Abraham, but what they were intended to mean by Him who declared them unto him.

The Issue

It appears then that the basic issue between the advocates of the Biblical and the Critical conceptions of Prophecy can be reduced to this all-important question. Are we to accept the situation, the scope, and the meaning which the Bible assigns to the predictions which it records, insofar as these are definitely stated, and to determine our conception of the nature of prophecy in conformity with the requirements and implications of the Biblical data? Or must we disregard the Biblical situation entirely, reject the statements of the Bible as to authorship, situation, and scope and assign to each utterance the situation which seems to suit it best, *it being assumed that the element of prediction is to be allowed to figure only very little if at all in deciding the question as to the identity of the speaker or the situation which was the occasion of his words?* It is the *Biblical* situation of such prophecies as have been discussed, and the *Biblical* fulfilment of these prophecies, which leads inevitably to the traditional belief that *pre*diction is an important element in prophecy. It has been the aim of the critics for many years to discredit and destroy this belief. And the extremes to which they are forced to go in order to accomplish this end are the clearest evidence that the traditional view of prophecy is the truly Biblical one. We meet this problem again and again as we study the prophetical books of the Old Testament, but nowhere more clearly and unavoidably than in the Book of Isaiah.

CHAPTER III

THE UNITY OF THE BOOK OF ISAIAH

The first and most obvious reason for regarding Isaiah as the author of the book which for centuries has borne his name is the heading: "The vision of Isaiah the son of Amoz, which he saw concerning Judah and Jerusalem in the days of Uzziah, Jotham, Ahaz, *and* Hezekiah, kings of Judah" (1:1). This heading is significant for several reasons. First of all, there is the fact that every one of the fifteen books which compose the collection known as the "Latter Prophets" commences with a heading. These books vary greatly in length and in style of composition; and the headings also vary greatly in form. But all agree in at least stating the *name* of the prophet whose utterances are contained in the book at the head of which each is placed. The briefest of them all is "The vision of Obadiah." Several add the name of the prophet's father, e.g., "Joel the son of Pethuel," or his status, "Habakkuk, the prophet, Ezekiel . . . the priest," or the city or district from which he came, "Micah, the Morash-tite, Nahum, the Elkoshite." All but three indicate the time or period in which the prophet prophesied. And in the case of four (Isaiah, Jeremiah, Hosea, Micah), it is stated that this ministry covered a considerable period, the reigns of three or four kings. But every book has a heading and every heading gives at least a name. In some of the books there are more or less frequent subordinate headings or datings. These appear most frequently in Jeremiah and Ezekiel. But the little book of Haggai has three such headings. In Isaiah, aside from the historical section (chaps. 36-39) there are only comparatively few subordinate headings (2:1; 6:1; 7:1; 13:1; 14:28; 16:13; 20:1) which mention the name of the prophet or give the time of the utterance. The twelve chapters (24-35) which follow the "Burdens" are entirely lacking in headings. In fact chap. 24 begins as abruptly as does chap. 40. For a distinct prophecy or series of prophecies by an unnamed prophet to begin at this point or elsewhere, without any heading whatsoever would be entirely contrary to analogy. It would mean that a collection of anonymous prophecies nearly half as long as the collection known as "The Twelve" had been included among the Writing Prophets. Obadiah, Joel, Nahum, Habakkuk are tiny books as compared with Isa. 40-66. But not one of them is anonymous. The names

39

"Obadiah," or "Joel, the son of Pethuel" may mean little to us. But at least their names are given. A "great Unknown," as the author of this group of chapters, or several such Unknowns, would be an anomaly. It is only by dividing up Micah, Zechariah and other of the Prophets that the critics succeed in producing an analogy to support their theory that the Fifteen known writing prophets include in their number and as perhaps the greatest of them all one, or even more than one, "unknown," because unnamed prophet.

Furthermore, there is no manuscript evidence to show that the entire 66 chapters do not constitute a single whole. This has recently been strikingly illustrated by the discovery of a very ancient "Isaiah Scroll."[1] For in it chapter 40 begins on the very last line of the column which contains 38:9-39:8. The last words on the one column are "cry unto her"; and the first words on the next column are "that her warfare is accomplished." Obviously the scribe was not conscious of the alleged fact that an important change of situation, involving an entire change of authorship begins with chapter 40. If this manuscript dates from about the middle of the 2nd century B.C., it is an early witness in favor of the unity of the entire book. For it probably carries us back nearly to the time when the LXX version of the Prophets was made.[2]

This new evidence is gratifying, both for its own sake and also because it encourages us to hope that other and still more important discoveries may be made in the future. But it does not really alter the situation as to the question of the unity of Isaiah.[3] For the critics have all along been prepared to admit that the theory of multiple authorship which they regard as

---

[1] This scroll was discovered in 1947 in a cave in the Judean hills near the Dead Sea. It is now available in photographic reproduction (*The Dead Sea Scrolls of St. Mark's Monastery*, 1950, vol. i). *The Bulletin of the American Schools of Oriental Research* (beginning with No. 110) supplies much information regarding it. It is not dated; and its age must be determined largely if not entirely from the style of writing and from the jars (pre-Herodian) in which it and other scrolls had been preserved. Palaeographic experts with few exceptions appear to be agreed that the scrolls are very old. If the date assigned by Albright and other competent scholars (*cir.* 150 B.C.) should prove to be correct, this manuscript is by a thousand years the earliest manuscript of an entire book of the Hebrew Old Testament.

[2] The LXX version was commenced in the 3rd cty. B.C. The great codices which contain it date, the earliest of them, from about five hundred years later. Kenyon regards the Chester Beatty Papyrus of Isaiah as dating "apparently from the first half of the second century" (*The Text of the Greek Bible*, 1937).

[3] According to Cheyne "critics in general are agreed that the final redaction of the Book of Isaiah must have been anterior to the composition of Ecclesiasticus (probably about 180 B.C.), because of the description of Isaiah's wide range as a prophet in Ecclus. 48:22-25" (*Encyclop. Biblica*, 2189).

one of the most assured results of modern critical study is a comparatively recent one, and that it is largely if not solely the result of that modern theory regarding prophecy which they claim to have discovered, a theory which largely eliminates prediction from prophecy. According to Davidson, "For about twenty-five centuries no one dreamt of doubting that Isaiah the son of Amoz was the author of every part of the book that goes under his name."[4] This is a most significant admission. The twenty-five centuries referred to cover the entire period from the lifetime of Isaiah to the emergence of the critical theory of multiple authorship about the beginning of the 19th century. This means that from the time of Isaiah until about 150 years ago, no one "dreamt" that in the Book of Isaiah itself, or in the rest of the Old Testament, or in the New Testament, or in the extra-Biblical sources, any evidence was to be found that Isaiah did not write "every part of the book that goes under his name." This is, we repeat, a most significant admission. The writer of all or the greater part of chapters 40-66 was certainly one of the greatest of the prophets. But if he was not Isaiah the son of Amoz, he was already in Old Testament times, and has continued to be to the present day, the Great Unknown; and to call him both "great" and "unknown" only serves to make the mystery of his anonymity the more remarkable. "Deutero" and "Trito" when prefixed to the name of Isaiah have no more significance than the x and y of an algebraic equation. They are merely symbols for unknowns the value of which is still to be determined.[5]

The fact that the Old Testament knows nothing of the existence of this great prophet of the exilic and early post-exilic period is a serious objection to the acceptance of this now popular theory. Jeremiah, Zephaniah, Ezekiel, Daniel, Haggai and Zechariah, prophesied in this period and are known to us by name. Yet that prophet whom many would regard as the greatest of them all is the Great Unknown. This is extremely unlikely, to say the least. It also lacks historical evidence to support it.[6]

[4] *Op. cit.*, p. 244. G. A. Smith described it as "the almost universally accepted tradition." The exceptions are so few that they may be said to prove the rule.

[5] E.g., J. Paterson tells us: "We have no knowledge of the personal life of this prophet; he is wholly anonymous" (*The Goodly Fellowship of the Prophets*, 1948, p. 192). The Great Unknown is still unknown!

[6] It has been claimed that the anonymity of Isa. 40-66 would be no more remarkable than that of the Book of Job. But the cases are not similar. Job contains no prophecies, whose authorship, date, or situation require determining; and while several other books of the Bible show indications of familiarity with Job, there is no quotation anywhere which names Job as its source.

The earliest *extra-Biblical* evidence is that of Ecclesiasticus (cir. 180 B.C.). There we read regarding Isaiah that "He saw by an excellent spirit what should come to pass at the last, and he comforted them that mourned in Sion. He shewed what should come to pass for ever, and secret things or ever they came" (Ecclus. 48:24f.). The words, "and he comforted them that mourn in Sion," naturally suggest Isa. 40:1 and 61:2f. and may be regarded as presupposing the entire Book of Consolation to be Isaianic; and the reference to the disclosure of future events suggests 48:3-7 and other passages which stress prediction and fulfilment.

The attitude of the *New Testament* is very significant. Isaiah is quoted *by name* about twenty times, which is more often than all the other "writing prophets" taken together. Furthermore, in those books where he is so quoted most frequently, citations are made from both parts of the book. Matthew quotes Isaiah by name six times, three times from the first part and three from the second.[7] Paul in Romans quotes Isaiah five times by name, and from both parts of the book.[8] John, while quoting less frequently, cites 53:1 and 6:10 in consecutive verses as "Isaiah" (Jn. 12:38f.). Luke tells us that "the book of the prophet Isaiah" was delivered to Jesus in the synagogue at Nazareth (4:17) and that He found there the passage which begins with the words, "The Spirit of the Lord is upon me" (61:1) and read from it. Furthermore, all four of the Gospels quote more or less extensively from Isa. 40:3f. as having its fulfilment in the ministry of John the Baptist (Mt. 3:3; Mk. 1:3; Lk. 3:4-6; Jn. 1:23); and in all of them the quotation is stated to be from "Isaiah the prophet." Luke is particularly precise, for he introduces his quotation with the words, "in the book of the words of Isaiah the prophet."[9] In Acts 8:30 we are told that the Ethiopian eunuch, when approached by Philip, was reading "Isaiah the prophet," and that the passage of Scripture was the one we know as 53:7f. Such evidence indicates with sufficient clearness that none of the New Testament writers "dreamt" that the name Isaiah was of doubtful or ambiguous meaning. Such facts as these should carry great weight with

---

[7] Cf. Mt. 3:3 (Isa. 40:3), 4:14 (Isa. 9:1f), 8:17 (53:4), 12:17-21 (42:1-4), 13:14 (Isa. 6:9f.), 15:7 (Isa. 29:13).

[8] Cf. Rom. 9:27 (Isa. 10:22), 9:29 (Isa. 1:9), 10:16 (Isa. 53:1), 10:20 (Isa. 65:1), 15:12 (Isa. 11:10).

[9] In Mark the quotation from Isaiah is preceded by one from Malachi (3:1). The reading "in Isaiah the prophet" is the reading of the best MSS (cf. RV). But the various reading, "in the prophets," is favored by the fact that two prophets are quoted.

every Christian who values the testimony of the New Testament.[10]

The significance of this evidence has been stated admirably by Alexander. After pointing out that these quotations of Isaiah by name are taken from twelve different chapters, seven of which are in the First Part and five in the Second, Alexander remarks: "Hence it is that in the older writers on Isaiah, even down to the middle of the eighteenth century, the place now occupied by *criticism,* in the modern sense, is wholly blank. No one, of course, thought it necessary to defend what had never been attacked, or to demonstrate what had never been disputed."[11]

It should be remembered then, that the basic question raised by the critics is not, how many Isaiahs there were, but whether there were more Isaiahs than the one. The critics assume that the battle over the question of the unity of the book has long been decided in their favor.[12] Consequently, for them the only question that is open to debate is, How many? But for those who still believe that the testimony of "twenty-five centuries," a testimony which rests so plainly on the teachings of the Bible, both Old Testament and New Testament, is worthy of the most careful consideration, the great issue is still the unity of the entire book of Isaiah. And the evidence which has been briefly summarized above should certainly not be ignored or lightly brushed aside.

THE CRITICAL ATTITUDE TO THE BOOK OF ISAIAH

Without attempting to enter in detail into the history of the critical interpretation of the Book of Isaiah, the most important steps which have distinguished it must now be briefly referred

---

[10] The attempt to set aside this evidence on such grounds as the following: (1) that none of these citations is made "by Our Lord Himself," (2) that none of them are in answer to the question, "Did Isaiah write chs. 40-66 of the book called by his name?" (3) that Isaianic authorship is not "involved" in the argument (cf. G. A. Smith, *Isaiah,* ii. 6) shows how hard put to it the critics are to avoid the natural implications of these quotations from "Esaias the prophet." Were such tests applied to the citations that are added as documentation in the margins of many scholarly books, the value of such references would be greatly reduced or destroyed!

[11] *Op cit.* i. xxv.

[12] In his Schweich Lectures on *The Composition of the Book of Isaiah* (1909), Kennett declared at the outset that "To argue at length that the book of Isaiah is not all the work of Isaiah the son of Amoz, but a composite document would be but to slay the slain" (p. 2). In the *General Introduction and Commentary* on the Old Testament edited by Alleman and Flack (1948), the statement is made: "Today practically all reputable scholars accept the Exilic origin of Deutero-Isaiah" (p. 675).

to.[13] First of all it is to be observed that the expression "Two Isaiahs," as a popular summing up of the conclusions of Criticism, is decidedly misleading. For it was made clear very early in the presentation of the new theory that, for the critics, the problem was a complicated one, which involved both Parts of the Book of Isaiah. Thus, Gesenius who defended the unity of "Second Isaiah" as an exilic document, assigned chaps. 13-14 in the First Part to about the same date as the Second Part. Davidson, toward the close of the last century summed up the critical consensus as follows:

"The portions of the Book of Isaiah which have been denied to be Isaiah's are these: *first,* the whole of the great prophecy of the Restoration, chaps. 40-66, and, *second,* many sections in the first 39 chapters, such as 13-14:23, 21:1-10, (chap. 23) 24-27, 34-35, and 36-39. The parts admitted to be genuine are chaps. 1-12, 15-20, part of 21, 22, 28-33,—in all, about 26 or 27 chapters out of a total of 66."[14]

As to the basis and warrant for this denial of about three-fifths of the Book to Isaiah, Davidson tells us :

"The general canon on which these conclusions are based is this: That a prophetic writer always makes the basis of his prophecies the historical position in which he himself is placed. This is not an *a priori* principle but is one gathered from careful observations, made on those prophecies the age of which is known. And this principle is supported by another, which is also a conclusion drawn from observation, namely that the purpose of prophecy as exercised in Israel was mainly ethical, bearing on the life and manners of the people among whom the prophet lived."

The reader will observe that this "general canon" is substantially the same as that which was quoted at the outset of this study, the only difference being that Davidson points out that in speaking to the people of his own time the aim of the prophet was ethical. This means that there is a marked tendency among the critics to identify prediction with the declaration of what we may call the moral inevitability of future events.

It is very important, therefore, to observe that, as has been made clear by the examples given in Chapter I, Davidson's state-

---

[13] The history of interpretation up to nearly the middle of the last century is dealt with by Alexander in the Introductions to the two volumes of his Commentary and also throughout the commentary itself. This feature is very valuable. In the series of articles referred to in Appendix III, Prof. Young has supplemented Alexander's discussion and brought it up to date. His comprehensive survey of a century of discussion of Isaiah and its problems should be read by all who wish to enter more fully into the subject. The subject is discussed from the "critical" standpoint in the *Introductions* by Driver, Oesterley and Robinson, and Pfeiffer, in G. B. Gray's *Commentary* in the *I.C.C.* series and in various other works.
[14] *Old Test. Prophecy,* p. 245.

ment is very far from being a correct one. It is not true that "the general canon" which plays such havoc with the unity of Isaiah "is gathered from careful observations, made on those prophecies the age of which is known." If such were actually the case, the position of the critics would be a very strong one. But the situation is quite different as we have seen. And it is just because the critics refuse to do full justice to this evidence, and to other facts which have already been presented, but insist in ignoring it or forcing it by drastic manipulation to conform to their theory, that their solution of the problem of Isaiah is still opposed and rejected by multitudes of Christians. And it is not necessary to assume the role of prophet, in order to assert that no solution will ever gain general acceptance unless it does full justice to all the evidence.

For an example we turn to Isa. 13. This chapter has a heading which definitely assigns it to Isaiah the son of Amoz. It contains a prophecy which definitely predicts the downfall of Babylon which did not take place until long after Isaiah's time. If the title is accepted, we have here prediction, long range prediction, by the son of Amoz. Yet as Alexander points out Rosenmüller, Eichhorn, and Gesenius—all early advocates of the modern critical theory—did not hesitate to assign it to the close of the Exilic period, the position given it in Davidson's consensus. The genuineness of the heading cannot be assailed on textual grounds. To reject it on the ground that Isaiah the contemporary of Hezekiah could not have foretold the downfall of Babylon, is equivalent to sifting the evidence by the use of the very principle the validity of which it is or should be the aim of the critics to establish.

With regard to the conclusions of criticism as stated by Davidson, it should be noted that his statement of results applies only to the "moderates" among the critics. The "radical" critics reduce the total of genuine verses to about one-fifth of the whole, or approximately 262 verses in the First Part of the Book.[15] And this has been done on the basis of the general principles enunciated by Davidson. The only difference, or at least the only essential difference is that the radicals are more consistent and thorough-going in the application of these principles to the data before them.

Conspicuous among the "radical" scholars just referred to was Bernhard Duhm, whose name is especially associated with the theory of the "Trito"-Isaiah. This means that Duhm separated

_____
[15] Art. "Isaiah" by G. L. Robinson in *Internat. Stand. Bibl. Encycl.*, p. 1505.

chaps. 56-66 from the so-called Deutero-Isaiah (40-66) and assigned them to an author who wrote perhaps a century later. There has been much discussion as to whether "Trito-Isaiah" is the work of a single prophet or is to be assigned to several disciples of Deutero-Isaiah, whose work Trito-Isaiah is admitted to resemble in important respects.[16]

As a reaction to the theory of the Trito-Isaiah, a decidedly radical one, the "new interpretation" proposed by C. C. Torrey in 1928 deserves mention. Torrey claimed that in chaps. 40-66 the references to Babylon and to Cyrus are so few (only five) that if they are eliminated as later insertions, which he described as bungling or tendentious, practically the whole of chaps. 40-66 can be assigned to a writer who lived in Palestine and knew nothing about a Babylonian Captivity and a return from the same. Torrey dated chapters 40-66 about a century after the Restoration, which practically amounts to saying that he assigned to Trito-Isaiah the chapters which critics originally assigned to Deutero-Isaiah and which Duhm and others have divided between Deutero- and Trito-Isaiah. He held that the insertion of these Cyrus interpolations or glosses had had a disastrous effect on the interpretation of Isa. 40-66: "It had two inevitable results: to transform the sublime poetry of a seer into a somewhat bizarre fantasia on current events; and to disintegrate the book for careful readers, for only a small part of it could be forced into the historical framework created by the interpolators."[17]

Despite Torrey's scathing denunciation of what had come to be regarded as practically axiomatic in critical circles, viz. that Isa. 40-55 presupposes a situation at the close of the Exile and deals especially with the release and restoration under Cyrus the Persian, the usual Babylonian interpretation, as we may call it, has recently been worked out most elaborately by an eminent Assyriologist, Sidney Smith. Seeking as a historian to trace the course of the notable career of Cyrus, Smith remarks that "The sources for the history of the years 556-538 are an odd collec-

---

[16] On Trito-Isa., see Creelman, *Introd.*, pp. 208-12. It is worthy of note that while in 1892 G. A. Smith felt that among chaps. 54-59 "the unity of . . . Second Isaiah gives way," he nevertheless discussed chaps. 54-56:8 as a group, under the heading "On the eve of Return." In that connection he expressed the opinion that chaps. 56:9-57 and 59 are "evidently pre-exilic," and he held that "the opening verse" of 56:1-8 "attaches it very closely to the preceding prophecy" (pp. 397, 406). Ten years later in his article "Isaiah" in the *Hastings Bible Dictionary,* he was apparently willing to accept Duhm's analysis which begins Trito-Isaiah at 56:1 and to assign all of the last 11 chapters to a post-exilic date. For an informing discussion of Duhm's exposition of 56:1-8, cf. E. J. Young (as cited *W. T. J.* vol. x. pp. 31-45).

[17] C. C. Torrey, *The Second Isaiah, A New Interpretation* (1928), p. viii.

tion." At nearly the end of a rather meagre list of sources he places Isa. 40-55 and evaluates them in the following significant words: "Incomparably the most important contemporary documents are to be found in the prophecies in cc. xl-lv of the book of Isaiah."[18] And after discussing these "historical" materials in detail, he even gives the reader a "Chronological Arrangement and Analysis of the Prophecies" on the assumption that they are contemporary documents. By so doing he places the "prophet" in the very centre of the stirring events with which his "prophecies" are supposed to deal and makes him, like Churchill at the time of the London Blitz and the stormy times that followed it, the conscience, counsellor, and guide of a people in its time of crisis. In fact Deutero-Isaiah as envisaged by Smith represents exactly the conception of the role of the prophet quoted above. He is "a man of his own time" and he speaks "to the people of his own time" of matters of "importance" to them. His words concern the present or the imminent future. They have no reference at all to any "non-existent situation." Torrey and Smith thus illustrate that seesaw in opinion which has had so many illustrations in the course of the "critical" interpretation of the Prophets and of the Bible as a whole.

Mention should also be made of the treatment of Isaiah by the "Form Critics." Form Criticism is the attempt to determine, to classify, and to trace the history of the various literary types or patterns which are to be found in the Bible and to relate them to similar "forms" to be found in other literatures. It is claimed that such patterns as, for example, odes, hymns, war songs, love and marriage songs, proverbs, laws, oracles, stories, and sagas, have each a long literary history. It is further claimed that these patterns, having originated in primitive, pre-literary times, must originally have been quite brief. Consequently, the tendency of Form Criticism is to break up extended passages into fragments. Thus, a prominent advocate of this theory tells us regarding Isa. 40-55: "We will have to count in cc. 40-55 about 50 very small units—songs and sayings—, perhaps more, perhaps also fewer." This would break up these chapters into units averaging some six or seven verses each. It is claimed for example that "40:1-2, 40:3-5, 40:6-8 are certainly at least relatively independent pieces."[19] Such a disintegrative analysis not only destroys the unity and cohesion of such a wonderful chapter as Isa. 40. It also shows quite clearly the disastrous

---

[18] Sidney Smith, *Isaiah Chapters, XL-LV, Literary Criticism and History* (Schweich Lectures of 1940), p. 30.

[19] Eissfeldt, *Einleitung*, p. 381.

consequences of applying such a fragmentizing theory to the Bible as a whole. While, according to this school of interpretation, it may be possible to trace to some extent the history of a specific pattern and to determine whether it is found in early literature or not, specific dating must depend largely, and in many cases entirely, on the historical allusions contained in the individual specimen of the pattern. And since the critics insist on regarding the references to history in these chapters as references to *current* events and not as predictions of *future* events, Form Criticism has introduced no radical change into the general critical position.[20] It has, however, concerned itself to a considerable extent with the question whether these prophetic utterances were delivered by word of mouth to an actual audience. or whether they were written down and issued as "fly sheets" by the prophet, as occasion and circumstance demanded.

The Situation of Isaiah 40-66

These chapters are, as we have already remarked, the testing ground even as they have long been the battle ground of the two conceptions of prophecy which we are examining. For nowhere else in Scripture are the two questions of the *situation* of the prophet and the *scope* of his prophecies more constantly to the fore. They are appropriately called the "Book of Consolation" because they begin with the words, "Comfort ye, comfort ye my people," and give the glad assurance, "Cry unto her that her warfare is accomplished." How are these words to be understood?

According to the traditional view, the *situation* of the prophet is indicated in the concluding verses of chap. 39. In that chapter we read of the embassy of Merodach-baladan to Hezekiah, ostensibly to congratulate him upon his recovery from illness, but probably with the further aim of enlisting Hezekiah's support against their common foe, the mighty king of Assyria. Hezekiah does not hesitate to show these men all his resources. Isaiah apparently sees in this, as was the case with David's census-taking, a boastful leaning upon the arm of flesh which merits rebuke. So he declares to Hezekiah that the time is coming when Babylon will succeed in doing what Assyria had failed to do; and Israel will become subject to the king of Babylon. Hezekiah acquiesces in this prophetic utterance with the words, "Good is the word of the Lord which thou hast spoken." And he goes on to snatch this crumb of comfort from the ominous words of the prophet, "For there shall be peace and truth in my

---

[20] Sidney Smith, *op. cit.*, pp. 16f.

day." Whether Isaiah regarded this comment as suitable and adequate we cannot say with certainty. It might be taken as suggesting the *"Après nous le deluge!"* of a monarch of modern times. At least this much must be said: it holds out no comfort for, and expresses no sympathy with, those who are to suffer the calamities which Isaiah has just foretold. What more natural, then, than that the tender-hearted prophet, brooding over the calamities which it had been his painful duty as the Lord's prophet to declare to his king, and impressed with the inadequacy of Hezekiah's answer, should direct his gaze toward that future which seemed so weighted with disaster[21] and should hear the voice of his God saying to him: "Comfort ye, comfort ye my people"?[22]

If this important occasion with its ominous interpretation gives us the actual *situation* of the prophet, it is to be noted that we learn from the words which follow the *scope* of his message of comfort: "Cry unto her that her warfare is accomplished, that her iniquity is pardoned, that she hath received of the Lord's hand double for all her sins." There is a comprehensiveness in these words which at once makes it unnecessary for us, indeed it directly forbids us, to restrict them merely to the scope suggested by the situation which called them forth. The happy ending of the seventy-year captivity, which was brought about through the edict of Cyrus, was not, as history shows very plainly, the completion of the "warfare"[23] of the people of God. Cyrus was

---

[21] Cf. Hab. 2:1.

[22] The promise of 15 years of life to Hezekiah (39:5) indicates that his illness must have taken place about the time of Sennacherib's invasion of Judah in Hezekiah's "fourteenth year" (36:1), and was not improbably the result of it. The historical account given in chaps. 36-37 apparently speaks of two invasions, the first in 714 B.C., which is merely mentioned in 36:1 (cf. 2 Kgs. 18:13-16), the second in 701, which is described in detail and concludes with an account of Sennacherib's death. This might be called the 'Sennacherib Chronicle' since it deals with the career of this monarch insofar as it concerned Hezekiah and his kingdom from the time when as Crown Prince he first came against Judah in 714 to his death nearly 35 years later. Consequently the words, "in those days" with which chap. 38 begins carry us back in time to about the beginning of chap. 36 (the "fourteenth year") and introduce an incident whose importance consists mainly in the fact that it led up to the ominous prediction of the Babylonian Captivity recorded in chap. 39. So understood, this oracle concerning Babylon must have been made known to Isaiah more than a decade before the Rabshakeh incident which forms the major theme of chaps. 36-37. This makes its position immediately before chaps. 40-66 especially significant. For it indicates very definitely that chap. 39 describes the *occasion* of chaps. 40-66.

[23] "Warfare" is the usual rendering of the Hebrew word. But it is also used in the sense of "service" (e.g., Num. 4:23). In Jer. 27 the rule of Nebuchadnezzar is called a "service" (here the usual word is used), which Jeremiah urged the Jews to accept as the only way of safety and life. It was their refusal to *serve* the king of Babylon in their own land which led to their service in Babylon, a service which was particularly humiliating and grievous.

a glorious, but only an imperfect type, of One whose coming was destined to deliver Israel from a far more grievous bondage than that of Babylon. And the New Testament plainly teaches and the Christian Church has always believed that the Book of Consolation speaks, not only of Cyrus the "shepherd," but also of a greater than Cyrus, of the Servant of the Lord, whose coming has already been so plainly and so gloriously foretold in the Book of Immanuel (Isa. 7-12).[24] Consequently the two great themes, or we may say, personalities in Isaiah 40-66 are Cyrus and the Servant of the Lord.

For the question of the unity of Isaiah, the Cyrus prophecy is of prime importance, because if it belongs to the exilic period the unity of the book cannot be maintained. But the problem of the identity of the Servant is of much greater importance, because in the New Testament certain of the Servant passages are so definitely interpreted as fulfilled in the Lord Jesus Christ. The two questions of *situation* and *scope* apply equally to both, though not in exactly the same way; and our decision regarding the one will have important bearing on our decision regarding the other. We begin with Cyrus.

---

[24] Alexander pointed out a century ago that the then "ancient and still current doctrine that the main subject of these Prophecies throughout, is the restoration from the Babylonian exile . . . affords the whole foundation of the modern neological criticism and exegesis" (*op. cit.*, vol. ii, p. xiv).

CHAPTER IV

THE PROPHECIES REGARDING CYRUS

In dealing with the problem of Cyrus in Isa. 40-48, we observe three things which are important and significant.

1. Cyrus and his mission are *repeatedly* referred to. This topic is not confined to a single passage; we meet it seven or eight times in these chapters and in various ways.[1] Cyrus is first referred to in 41:2-5. He is not named, but it seems clear that "the righteous man" is Cyrus; and the description of his victorious career, though brief, is very vivid. It is followed by a reference to idolatry; and it would be tempting to find in vv. 6-7 an allusion to that intense, though sadly misdirected, religiosity of which Nabunaid, like Edward the Confessor, has often been cited as an illustration. For this ill-fated monarch was greatly interested in restoring the idol temples of Babylonia, more so perhaps than in strengthening her armies of defense. In v. 25 we have a further reference to Cyrus. But the allusion is much less definite and detailed than in vv. 2-5. In 43:14 there is a reference to the downfall of Babylon which is to be brought about by Cyrus. But the name of its conqueror is not yet given. The first mention of Cyrus by name occurs in 44:28. It forms the climax of an elaborate prophetic poem which we shall presently discuss in detail. This verse confines itself to what Cyrus will do for Israel, to the restoration of the cities of Judah, of Jerusalem, and of the temple. It introduces a message from the Lord to Cyrus, "his anointed," which stresses both the comprehensive nature of the mission of Cyrus and the fact that it is for the sake of His chosen people and for the extending of His glory and fame among the nations that the Lord has raised up Cyrus and commissioned him (45:1-7). After a brief digression which like 41:6-7 describes the nothingness of idols, Cyrus is again referred to in 45:13. The Lord has raised him up "in righteousness" (cf. 41:2) and declares, "He

---

[1] The passages usually regarded as referring to Cyrus are: 41:2*a*, 25; (43:14); 44:24-28; 45:1-5, 13; 46:11, 48:14f. Caspari regards 42:1-4, 5-9 as referring to Cyrus but they are usually interpreted as spoken of the Servant of the Lord (*Lieder und Gottessprüche der Rückwanderer,* 1934). Sidney Smith, *Isaiah XL-LV* finds in 54:16 a further reference or allusion to Cyrus (p. 107). He makes all the servant passages refer to Cyrus or to the prophet himself, except of course, where Israel is expressly mentioned. According to Kennett in its *"original* connexion" Isa. 61:1ff. "appears to have been a soliloquy put into the mouth of Cyrus" (*op. cit.,* p. 31). But he included it among the prophecies of the 2nd century (p. 85).

shall build my city and he shall let go my captives:" again the emphasis is on the deliverance of Israel. Two other passages follow, both of which are indefinite. The "ravenous bird" (46:11) who is further described as "the man of my counsel" probably refers to Cyrus and stresses the thought already presented in 45:1-5 that Cyrus' conquests will be bloody as well as peaceful. It might seem somewhat strange that, after the very definite references to Cyrus in 44:28f. in which he is named and his career so fully described, the reference here should be somewhat metaphorical and indefinite. Finally in 48:14f. we have a reference to the fall of Babylon which resembles 43:14; and here the language is so ambiguous that it is uncertain whether the words "loved him" refer to Cyrus or Israel.[2] If the latter, then this passage like 43:14 refers to Cyrus only by implication. It thus appears that the mention of Cyrus by name in 44:28f. is the culmination of a cycle of Cyrus prophecies which runs through this entire group of chapters. Or, to use a different figure, this group of passages is like a wave which beginning with 41:2-5 mounts higher and higher till it reaches 44:28f. and then recedes at 48:14f. practically to its starting-point.

2. When we examine these passages somewhat more closely we observe a second important feature. It is the *vivid* way in which the central figure is introduced and his mission described. He is spoken *of* (44:28, 45:1) and spoken *to* (45:2-6). And there is also the rather startling commingling of past, present, and future, which appears elsewhere in the Book of Isaiah. Thus, in 45:1-5 the conquests of Cyrus are represented as future; and in v. 13 we read "he shall build my city and send forth my captivity" (cf. 48:14). On the other hand in 43:14 we read "I have sent to Babylon" and the command is given, "Go ye forth from Babylon . . . Say ye, The LORD has redeemed his servant Jacob," which suggests that the city has already fallen to the armies of Cyrus. We note further that the poem in 44:24-28 is

---

[2] The natural rendering is "the LORD loves him, he will do his pleasure on Babylon and his right arm (shall be on) the Chaldeans." If the "him" is Israel, it is best to regard what follows as describing what the LORD will do to prove His love to His people. If the "him" is Cyrus, it is natural to regard him as the agent in executing the pleasure of the LORD. The rendering "One that loves Yahweh will carry out" (Orelli), is possible. But it requires a change in the "pointing" of the Hebrew Text (reading the verb as participle instead of as perfect) which is not necessary. Such a change not only makes Cyrus the subject, but puts the emphasis on his love of Israel's God. The literal rendering would then be: "The LORD— his lover will do His pleasure," *i.e.*, "He who loves the LORD will do His pleasure." This rendering will only appeal to those who believe that Cyrus actually became a true worshipper of Jehovah, a view which as we shall see presently is not taught in Scripture nor supported by secular history.

introduced by the words: "Sing, O ye heavens: for the LORD hath done *it*: shout, ye lower parts of the earth: break forth into singing, ye mountains, O forest, and every tree therein: for the LORD hath redeemed Jacob and he will glorify himself in Israel." A deliverance already fully accomplished could not be more exultantly described. Yet other passages represent it as still future. Similarly we observe that the challenging question of 41:2f., "Who raised up from the east the righteous one?" is speedily followed by the question-answer, 'Who hath wrought and done *it*, calling the generations from the beginning? I the LORD, the first, and with the last; I am he." The terrified nations have no answer to the questions raised by the coming and career of Cyrus. They could neither anticipate it, nor can they explain it. It is the LORD, who called the generations from the beginning, that has raised up Cyrus to perform His counsel. The implication is clear that, as is asserted again and again in these chapters, the God of Israel has not only raised up Cyrus but has declared His purpose to do this long before Cyrus appeared upon the stage of history: "I have even from the beginning declared *it* to thee; before it came to pass I showed *it* thee: lest thou shouldest say, Mine idol hath done them, and my graven image, and my molten image, hath commanded them" (48:5, cf. 45:21). Here three common names for the idols of the heathen are brought together to emphasize the fact that the idols cannot predict things to come: their devotees can only pretend that they have done so when the events they could not foresee have taken place. Consequently, it is by declaring them long in advance, long before the keenest eye of statesman or diviner can see even the little cloud like the hand of a man upon the horizon, that the LORD God of Israel establishes His pre-eminent claim to be the Sovereign and Governor of the whole creation which He has made. Yet they may also be spoken of as if the prophet were witnessing or had witnessed their actual occurrence!

3. In the third place, we note a *complexity* or two-sidedness, if we may call it that, in the figure of Cyrus, which is remarkable and significant. On the one hand this mighty warrior, who is to be the great instrument in the Lord's hand for the deliverance of His people, is described as one who "calls" or "will call" on the name of the Lord, which might suggest invoking His aid as a true worshipper (41:25)[3] and he is given titles

---

[3] Sidney Smith would render "He shall summon in *My* Name" (*op. cit.*, p. 51) which like the AV rendering implies that Cyrus regards himself as commissioned for his task by the God of Israel.

which not only suggest that he is an Israelite, but might even be taken to mean that he is that Coming One, for whom Israel had long been looking (e.g., Deut. 18:14ff.) and who is the great theme of Messianic prophecy. He is called "my shepherd," a title which is given to the theocratic king in Jer. 23 and Ezek. 34, as well as to that future Ruler who in these very passages is set in contrast with all false shepherds, both Israelitish and foreign. The Lord also refers to Cyrus as "his anointed" *(Messiah)*, a title which is given to both kings and priests in Israel and which becomes the peculiar title of Him who is to reign as "a priest upon his throne" (Zech. 6:13).

This description of Cyrus has given great offense to a number of interpreters. Some of them hold that such titles are impossible and even blasphemous as applied to a Gentile and heathen king; and they make drastic attempts to eliminate them or explain them away.[4] Others hold that the use of these titles indicates that Cyrus was at first hailed as the Messiah by the prophet, and that it was only when he failed to realize the Messianic ideal and attributed his triumphs to Marduk instead of to Jehovah, that the prophet realized his mistake and transferred his hopes for the future of Israel and of humanity to the "Servant."[5] Neither of these extreme positions is justified. It is, of course, quite possible that there were Jews in the Captivity who were venturing, in the light of the prophet's words, to hope that Cyrus would declare himself a worshipper of the God of Israel, and who were consequently greatly chagrined and disappointed when he did not do so, but instead, and perhaps for political expediency, did honor to the gods of Babylon of whom the prophet had so often spoken with the utmost scorn and contempt. But it is a mistake to charge the prophet with sharing or encouraging this illusory hope. We must look on the other side of the picture.

In spite of and in striking contrast to the exalted titles which are given to Cyrus by the prophet, it is definitely pointed out

---

[4] W. A. Wordsworth (*En Roeh*, 1939) has gone almost as far as has Torrey (*The Second Isaiah*, 1928) in the attempt to eliminate Cyrus from Isa. 44:28f. His argument is quite as theoretical and "critical," despite the fact that he writes as a defender of the unity of Isaiah, while Torrey writes as a free-lance critic.

[5] For a brief account of this view cf. Sidney Smith (*op. cit.*, pp. 18f., 106f.). Smith refers to Staerk, Hempel, Mowinckel, and others as holding that there was such "an opposition between two stages in the prophet's career." A fuller discussion is given by Ploeg (*Les Chants du Serviteur de Jahvé*, pp. 162-8), who for quite different reasons than those advanced by Smith (Ploeg adopts the Messianic interpretation) rejects this "disappointment" theory. It is only when the prophet is made the *contemporary* of Cyrus that this theory becomes at all plausible.

that Cyrus is a foreign conqueror. He is not raised up out of "the midst" of Israel (Deut. 18:15, 18). He is raised up "from the east" (41:2), from "the north," from the "rising of the sun" (v. 25), from "a far country" (46:11). The fact that he is not an Israelite seems to be especially stressed. This is important because the kingship in Israel was definitely Israelitish (Dt. 17:15) and Davidic (2 Sam. 7). A foreign king, save as scourge and oppressor (e.g., Isa. 10:5-19) or as protector and helper (Isa. 49:23) was not within the scheme of the Theocracy, but definitely opposed to it. So the emphasis on the fact that he is not an Israelite indicates that in the case of Cyrus as in that of Nebuchadnezzar, who is called Jehovah's "servant" by Jeremiah (25:9; 27:6; 43:10), the words "shepherd" and "anointed" are not used in the theocratic sense.[6]

Still more important is the fact that in the very passage in which the prophet describes the glorious career of Cyrus in most glowing colors, we meet a statement which is made twice over as if for tragic emphasis: "though thou hast not known me," which, to bring out the Hebrew idiom, might be para-phrased, "hast not known and dost not know." It used to be argued that Cyrus became a true worshipper of the God of Israel. But the Biblical evidence does not warrant this suppo-sition and the archaeological evidence which has been brought to light indicates that, whether from conviction or for political reasons, Cyrus recognized and worshipped Jehovah only as one of many gods.[7] For in the *Cylinder* inscription he gives to Bel

---

[6] The word "anointed" as used of Cyrus need mean no more than that his rule over Persia and Babylon was authorized and approved by the God of Israel, that he was the Lord's anointed for the purpose of performing all His "pleasure." Hazael was in this sense the Lord's "anointed" (1 Kgs. 19:15), despite the fact that like Jehu, his own aims were selfish and cruel and un-worthy of his "anointing" (2 Kgs. 8:10-15). The use of the word "anoint" certainly implies that there was a true sense in which so utterly unmessianic a king as Hazael could be called "the Lord's anointed." If so, its use of Cyrus while remarkable and unusual would be eminently appropriate. Similarly "shep-herd" is used of that antithesis of the true (Davidic) shepherd who is described in Zech. 11:16.

[7] The tragedy in the career of Cyrus appears in these words, "though thou hast not known me," especially in view of the "that thou mightest know" of v. 3. For in this chapter even more than elsewhere in chaps. 40-48 the sole and exclusive Deity of Jehovah is repeatedly stressed. Note the immediate context: "I am the LORD and there is none else, there is no God beside me: I girded thee, though thou hast not known me" (cf. also vv. 6, 14, 18, 21, 22). According to the words of the *Cyrus Cylinder,* Cyrus was at least a political polytheist. "May all the gods," says Cyrus, "whom I have brought into their cities, pray daily before Bel and Nabu for long life for me, and may they speak a gracious word for me and say to Marduk, my lord, 'May Cyrus, the king who worships thee, and Cambyses his son . . .'" (cf. Finegan, *Light from the Ancient East,* p. 191). Consequently the correct rendering of Ezra 1:3 is "and build the house of

and Nebo the glory for his peaceful conquest of Babylon.[8]

THE TRADITIONAL INTERPRETATION

Since the name of Cyrus does not appear in the New Testament and the passages which mention him by name are not quoted or referred to in it, the explicit testimony of the Jewish historian Josephus (1st century) is very valuable and instructive. Like the New Testament writers, Josephus makes several references to Isaiah by name and he clearly ascribes passages from both parts of the book to him. Thus, he found in the erection of a temple and altar in Egypt by the high priest Onias the fulfillment of "an ancient prediction made by [a prophet] whose name was Isaiah" (apparently referring to 19:19-25), "about 600 years before."[9] He also referred expressly to the Cyrus Prophecy and attributed it to Isaiah. The passage is so important that, although familiar, it deserves to be quoted in full. After referring to Jeremiah's prophecy of restoration and prosperity after the Seventy Years should be accomplished,[10] Josephus goes on to say:

Jehovah God of Israel (he is the god who is in Jerusalem)" (cf. ARV margin). Apparently Cyrus recognized Jehovah as the God of Israel and was quite ready to foster his worship in order that the Jews, together with the other nations in his great empire might "pray for the life of the king and of his sons" (Ezra 6:10). Farther than this he did not go. He did not know Jehovah as Isaiah did, as the *only* God. Consequently we must be prepared to say that he did not really *know* him at all. Hence the tragedy of the words "I girded thee, though thou has not known me" in their refrain-like setting, "I am the LORD and there is none else."

The question may well be raised as to the extent to which Cyrus was himself responsible for the wording of this inscription, or whether perhaps it represents an attempt of the priestly party in Babylon to retrieve their position and gain the good will of the conqueror by representing Cyrus as the patron of their gods. Cyrus' successors on the throne pay tribute chiefly or exclusively to Ahuramazda for their successes. The exact date of Zoroaster is uncertain. Cyrus may have been a Mazdian and have accepted the monotheistic trend of the old Persian religion. But it seems clear that for political reasons he recognized and favored the religions of the peoples he conquered.

[9] Josephus, *Wars*, VII, x, 3. The familiar Whiston translation is used in the quotations.

[10] Ezra 1:1 and Dan. 9:1 mention Jeremiah because it is the *time* of the deliverance which is particularly stressed in both passages: the *first year* of Cyrus (=the *first year* of Darius as vice-king?) is the *seventieth year* of the Captivity (2 Chr. 36:21). Therefore God stirs up the spirit of Cyrus. Isaiah's prophecy concerns not the time but the agent, Cyrus, and has its fulfilment in the Edict which is quoted in both Ezra and Josephus. The edict naturally refers only to the God of heaven, who is the God of Jerusalem, and makes no mention of Isaiah, since a reference to him by name would be quite meaningless to any of Cyrus' subjects except Jews and Israelites. A further reason may be found in court etiquette. Just as Pharaoh, after learning from Joseph that his family have arrived in Egypt, informs Joseph of the fact, as if knowledge of it had come to him, the all-wise Pharaoh, directly and not through his viceroy, so Cyrus refers to the commission he has received from the God of Israel without mentioning in any way the human agency through whom it came to him.

"And these things God did afford them; for he stirred the mind of Cyrus, and made him write this throughout all Asia: 'Thus saith Cyrus the king: Since God Almighty hath appointed me to be king of the habitable earth, I believe that he is that God which the nation of the Israelites worship; for indeed he foretold my name by the prophets, and that I should build him a house at Jerusalem, in the country of Judea.'

"This was known to Cyrus by his reading the book which Isaiah left behind of his prophecies*; for this prophet said that God had spoken thus to him in a secret vision: 'My will is, that Cyrus, whom I have appointed to be king over many and great nations, send back my people to their own land, and build my temple.' This was foretold by Isaiah one hundred and forty years before the temple was demolished. Accordingly, when Cyrus read this, and admired the Divine power, an earnest desire and ambition seized upon him to fulfil what was so written; so he called for the most eminent Jews that were in Babylon and said to them, that he gave them leave to go back to their own country, and to rebuild their city Jerusalem, and the temple of their God, for that he would be their assistant, and that he would write to the rulers and governors that were in the neighborhood of their country of Judea, that they should contribute to them gold and silver for the building of the temple, and besides that, beasts for their sacrifices."[11]

From this it appears, not merely that Josephus regarded the Cyrus Prophecy as having been uttered by Isaiah, but that he found in the fact that this prediction was uttered "one hundred and forty years" before Nebuchadnezzar destroyed the temple and nearly two hundred years before Cyrus captured Babylon convincing proof of that "Divine power," which made it appeal especially to the mighty monarch whose glorious career it so plainly foretold. How great importance Josephus attached to the predictive element in prophecy is made clear by the fact that in the case of the one utterance he points out that it was uttered "about six hundred years" and of the other "one hundred and forty years" (and more) before the fulfilment took place. Indeed, he tells us that, by dependence on Isaiah the prophet, Hezekiah "inquired and knew all future events" and also that Isaiah "wrote down all his prophecies and left them in books, that their accomplishment might be judged of from the events by posterity."[12] These statements make it very clear that Josephus believed that many of Isaiah's prophetic utterances were predictions which had reference to the future, even to a remote future, and that Josephus saw in this fact and in their fulfilment in history the singular and conclusive proof of their divine origin and authority. It also appears that Josephus believed that many of these utterances were addressed to and intended for the men of future generations (Isa. 8:16-22; Dan. 12:4-9) and that it was

---

[11] *Antiq.* XI.i.1f. * The best Mss. add here "two hundred and ten years earlier."
[12] *Ibid.,* X. ii. 2.

for this very reason that they were made a matter of record by the prophet himself (Hab. 2 :2f.).

Josephus' testimony is especially valuable for two reasons. The first is that it clearly represents the historical consensus, as we may call it, regarding the Book of Isaiah to which Davidson referred. Obviously Josephus was one of those who never "dreamt" that the entire book had any other author than that Isaiah the son of Amoz who prophesied in the days of king Hezekiah. The second reason is that it is made so clear by Josephus' statements that the acceptance of his view as to the "situation" of the prophecies carries with it, as its inevitable and highly important corollary, a very definite conception as to the true nature of prophecy. Josephus definitely repudiates that conception of prophecy which makes the prophet always "a man of his own time" and restricts his message to "the men of his own time" and to matters of "importance" to them, and therefore regards it as axiomatic that a prophet could not deal with a "non-existent" situation. He repudiates we may say in advance the main contentions of the modern critics; and he finds in these very things which are to them the insuperable obstacle to the Isaianic authorship of this prophecy the most convincing proof of its "Divine power." The special importance of Josephus' testimony is, therefore, that it represents in general that conception of prophecy and that interpretation of the Prophetical Books of the Old Testament which remained practically unchallenged by Christians until nearly the beginning of the last century.[13]

THE CRITICAL INTERPRETATION

Since the theory held by the critics as to the nature of prophecy differs so radically from the one we have just described, it is inevitable that their conclusions as to the situation of Isaiah

---

[13] "A special ground on which the denial of the genuineness of the last twenty-seven chapters rests is the mention of Cyrus by name (44:28; 45:1). So also Josiah was foretold by name (1 Kgs. 13:2). If predictive prophecy is possible, if it was ever uttered by holy men taught by the Holy Spirit, then the name of Cyrus could have been penned by ˙aiah. Otherwise the words, as they stand, were not uttered until nearly two hundred years after Isaiah. The church has always believed in predictive prophecy and in the inspiration of Isaiah" (Article "Isaiah," in *A Dictionary of the Bible* by John D. Davis, 4th edition, concluding paragraph). "External evidence is all in favour of the unity of the book. Until within the last hundred years, the unhesitating belief of the Jewish and Christian Church (with the doubtful exception of the Jewish writer Aben Ezra in the twelfth century A.D.) as well as the implicit authority of Christ and His Apostles, has assigned the whole to Isaiah the son of Amoz" (Angus-Green, *Cyclopedic Handbook of the Bible*, p. 499f.). In 1879 Delitzsch described the mention of Cyrus as the "nerve" of "the settled opinion of the critics" (*Jesaia*, 3d German edition, p. 411).

40-66 and of the Cyrus Prophecies in particular should also be markedly different. According to them, the contents of the prophecies themselves very clearly indicate their situation: "their circumstance of exile is taken for granted; there is a most vivid and delicate appreciation of their present fears and doubts, and to these the deliverer Cyrus is not only named, but introduced as an actual and notorious personage already upon the midway of his irresistible career."[14] This means, of course, that the prophet is not dealing with a "non-existent situation." His words presuppose and describe exilic conditions; and this indicates that he is living in the midst of them. The exilic "atmosphere" must give us the actual historical setting or situation of the prophecies. Furthermore, the mention of Cyrus by name and the assigning to him of a task which is as difficult as it is important must mean that he is "already well-known" as an irresistible warrior. He is not a forlorn hope. He is not a remote and untried possibility. He is "on the point of striking at Babylon," and of doing this "with all the prestige of unbroken victory!" So runs the argument. And statements to similar effect can be found in practically every book which adopts the "critical" view regarding Isa. 40-66. The only change in the attitude of the critics in recent years has been that this position is now no longer regarded by them as one which requires proof, but rather as one which needs only to be stated in order to be accepted as self-evident and axiomatic. The extreme to which this view can be carried is illustrated by the statement quoted above, according to which, for the historian, "Incomparably the most important contemporary documents are to be found in the prophecies in cc. xl-lv of the book of Isaiah."[15]

---

[14] G. A. Smith, *The Book of Isaiah*, vol. ii., p. 9. This writer tells us further: "Cyrus, in short, is not presented as a prediction, but as the proof that a prediction is being fulfilled. Unless he had already appeared in flesh and blood, and was on the point of attacking Babylon, with all the prestige of unbroken victory, a great part of Isa. 41-48 would be utterly unintelligible." For more recent statements to the same effect, see for example, F. C. Eiselen, *The Prophetic Books of the Old Testament*, vol. i (1923), pp. 209-12, J. Paterson, *The Goodly Fellowship of the Prophets* (1948), p. 193. It is to be noted, of course, that for most of the critics of the present time, Cyrus, having served the purpose of disproving the *early* date of Isa. 40-66, loses all significance for determining the *real* date of many passages in these chapters notably chaps. 56-66. Thus Kennett, in his Schweich Lectures, dated portions of Isa. 44-45 in the Maccabean period, despite the fact that he assigned 44:9-20, 24-28, 44:1-13 to the time of Cyrus.

[15] How thoroughly *contemporary* these prophecies become is indicated by the fact that Sidney Smith arranges the data contained in chaps. 40-55 in nine groups. He assigns them in chronological sequence to the period beginning "after the outbreak of hostilities between Cyrus and Nabonidus, shortly before the attack on the Babylonian governors in Northern Syria" and ending with the prophet's death, which he places after the fall of Babylon. These various docu-

It will be noted, of course, how greatly the *situation* which the critics assign to this prophecy reduces its *scope* by eliminating almost completely the predictive element from it. As the critics view the situation, the one who spoke these words of prophecy did not need to be a prophet to foresee that the fall of Babylon to Cyrus was inevitable. That was already so plainly written into the record of coming events, it was so obviously on the agenda, that he that ran could read it. Cyrus had "a record of unbroken victory" and was "on the point of attacking Babylon." The only thing which might be regarded as uncertain would be the question of Cyrus' attitude to the Jews. And it would be the most natural thing in the world for one who considered himself a spokesman of the Jewish exiles, to see in Cyrus a possible deliverer and to voice the hope, stating it in terms of positive conviction, that he would not only deliver them from the hated yoke of Babylon but even permit them to return to their own land and restore its desolations. In other words this interpretation of the Cyrus Prophecies is in entire accord with the basic principles regarding the nature of prophecy adopted by the critics.

The obvious fact that the critical interpretation of the prophecies regarding Cyrus empties them of all or most of their truly predictive character has been met in two ways by those critics who are prepared to maintain that there really is a predictive element in prophecy. On the one hand we are told that Cyrus is the *fulfilment* of other prophecies than those contained in Isa. 40-48. As examples of such prophecies, Jeremiah's prophecy of the Seventy Years is appealed to, or Habakkuk's prediction of the fall of Babylon.[16] But this is not a satisfactory answer. For it has to be admitted that no definite prediction of Cyrus, certainly no mention of him by name, is to be found anywhere in the Prophets, aside from these passages in Isaiah. So we are told, on the other hand, that the fact that there is nowhere a definite prediction of Cyrus, is to be explained in the light of

---

ments are all called "prophecies." This use of them has been aptly described by North in the following words: "Although Smith does not say so in so many words—the lectures were delivered early in 1941—the Prophet with his enthusiasm for Cyrus, was very much in the position of a leader of the underground movement in the as yet unbroken Babylonian Empire" (*The Suffering Servant*, p. 85). The historian is to be commended for using all the information which he can lay hands on in order to throw light upon a somewhat obscure period of ancient history. But it would seem to be obvious that such use of these prophetic utterances—as contemporary documents, "fly sheets" dealing with a constantly changing political situation—is the *reductio ad absurdum* of them as *predictive* prophecy.

[16] G. A. Smith, *op. cit.*, vol. ii., p. 11.

such passages as 48:6b-8 which speak of "new things" and "hidden things," things which Israel did not "know," things which the God of Israel is bringing to pass without any previous announcement. Cyrus' coming is such a "new" thing.[17] It will be noted, of course, that these two arguments cancel one another. If Cyrus' coming was really predicted by Jeremiah or another of the prophets, then it was not a "new thing." On the other hand, if it was a "new thing," it is a mistake to call it the fulfilment of prophecy. Yet certainly in a group of chapters in which the power of God to predict and fulfil is so stressed as it is here, it would be remarkable if so signal an event as the appearance of Cyrus were to be entirely unheralded.

Having discussed briefly, but we believe adequately, the reasons in so far as they involve predictive prophecy, that lead critical scholars to reject so emphatically the unity of Isaiah and the important role which the mention of Cyrus by name in 44:28f. plays in the bringing about of this result, we shall now proceed to examine this prophecy in detail, with a view to determining whether the prophecy itself supports the traditional or the critical interpretation which is given to it.

---

[17] *Ibid.*, p. 206f.

CHAPTER V

A PROPHETICAL POEM CELEBRATING THE TRANSCENDENCE OF THE LORD GOD OF ISRAEL[1]

The mention of Cyrus by name as the Lord's shepherd who will order the rebuilding of the cities of Judah and the restoration of Jerusalem and of the temple which is desolate is one of the most remarkable single phenomena in the entire book of Isaiah. It may properly be said of it that it either offers conclusive proof of the unique inspiration of the prophet who uttered it more than 140 years before its fulfilment or that it furnishes equally conclusive proof that this prophetic utterance and probably other and extended portions of the book we call "Isaiah" must date from a time long after the close of the ministry of the son of Amoz. At the risk of being accused of attempting to simplify the problem unduly, it may be said that if the Cyrus prophecy can be regarded as by Isaiah there is little if any warrant for denying to him the authorship of the entire book which passes under his name.

Such being the case it is highly important to observe the connection in which the name of Cyrus is introduced. For the mention of Cyrus by name, momentous as it is, is the climax, we might almost say merely the climax, of a unique poem which celebrates the transcendence of the God of Israel, His incomparable greatness, His absolute sovereignty in all the affairs of men. The poem of only five verses (44:24-28) is markedly chronological and it celebrates the transcendence of the God of Israel in the past, the present, and the future. It is a poem which gathers up the major themes of chapters 40-48 and presents them in a strikingly beautiful and impressive form.

THE SETTING OF THE POEM

The great aim of this group of chapters is to comfort Israel by declaring and demonstrating the true character of the God

[1] The interpretation of this prophecy which is presented in the following pages was first proposed by the present writer in an article entitled, "The Transcendence of Jehovah God of Israel" which appeared in the volume of *Biblical and Theological Studies* published in connection with the celebration of the Centennial of Princeton Theological Seminary in 1912. But aside from the fact that both set forth and defend the same view regarding the Cyrus Prophecy, the two discussions of the subject are quite distinct.

of Israel, His utter uniqueness, His incomparable greatness, His transcendence over all the works of His hands, His absolute control over the entire course of human history, and His wonderful nearness to His people as Saviour and Lord. The God of Israel is the Incomparable One. "To whom then will ye liken me, or shall I be equal" (40:25; cf. 40:18; 44:8; 46:5) is the challenge of the Holy One who is Israel's God. It is answered in two ways: by affirming His incomparable greatness and proving it by directing attention to His mighty acts, and by contrasting Him with the impotent idols of the heathen. He is the only God, the creator of all things, the preserver and bountiful benefactor of all who put their trust in Him. They are things of naught, the work of men's hands.[2] Idolatry is not only folly, it is positively silly and absurd. Both of these themes run through this entire group of chapters; and both reach their climax and appear in their sharpest and most amazing contrast in this one. Here the prophetic irony and scorn reaches its climax, as the prophet points out the utter stupidity of supposing that a man can cut down a tree of the forest, fashion an idol out of it, and use the rest as kindling wood to warm himself and to cook by (vss. 9-20). Hardly less impressive is the picture in chapter 46 of Bel and Nebo, the great gods of Babylon, whose images have been for centuries carried yearly in solemnly splendid procession through the streets of Babylon—these very same images loaded as "baggage" (*impedimenta*) upon the backs of weary beasts to go into captivity with a people they are impotent to save! How different is the God of Israel who has from the beginning carried His people on His bosom like a babe in arms and will yet "carry and deliver" them. Small wonder that the prophet follows such a contrast by repeating the challenge, "To whom will ye liken me and make me equal and compare me, that we may be like?"(46:5).

There is another feature of this annihilating comparison between the Incomparable God of Israel and the "vanities" of the heathen, which is especially to be noted. It is referred to

---

[2] 40:19f.; 41:7; 42:17; 44:9-20; 45:16, 21; 46:1-7; 48:5; cf. 47:13. The highest point to which idolatry can attain is described in 44:13, "The carpenter . . . maketh it after the figure of a man, according to the beauty of a man; that it may remain in the house." The human form is the loftiest *image* that man can form of God. But it is not in his body, but in his spirit, that man is made in the image of God. The true anthropomorphism described in Gen. 1:26 is interpreted in the whole course of Biblical revelation. The false anthropomorphism which is both the characterization and the condemnation of the ethnic religions is described with horrifying realism by Paul in Rom. 1:21-23. It is this which led the prophets to refer to idolatry and the vile practices associated with it as the "abominations" of the heathen (Isa. 44:19).

again and again in these chapters and emphasized as nowhere else in Scripture. It is the fact that the disclosure of things to come is the special and exclusive prerogative of Israel's God. Again and again in this group of chapters the LORD, through the lips of his prophet, challenges the idol-gods to *declare the things that are to come*.[3] Again and again it is pointed out that the Lord has both foretold and also fulfilled that which He has foretold. Thus, in 41:21-26 where this theme is discussed in some detail, this challenge is flung out to them: "Shew the things that are to come hereafter, that we may know that ye are gods." And in 48:3f., we are told that the reason for the foretelling of things to come by the God of Israel through his prophets is lest the people should say: "Mine idol hath done them, and my graven image, and my molten image, hath commanded them." Again and again it is pointed out that God alone knows and that He alone can reveal the future.[4] And because of this He invites inquiry regarding it: "Ask me of things to come concerning my sons, and concerning the work of my hands command ye me" (45:11). Certainly we might expect to find here in this group of chapters, if anywhere in the Bible, some signal proof of the validity of this transcendent claim which is made here so often by the God of Israel. And the remarkable poem which we are now to study furnishes such a proof.

THE INTRODUCTION

The prophetic poem of which the mention of Cyrus forms the impressive conclusion is introduced by the words: "Thus saith the LORD, thy redeemer, and he that formed thee from the womb." The words, "Thus saith the LORD," occur somewhat frequently in Isaiah and are widely distributed (e.g., 7:7 and 66:13).[5] Sometimes they are simply followed by a statement of what the Lord has said. But quite often they are accompanied by a descriptive phrase, as here by the words, "thy Redeemer and

---

[3] The word rendered "declare" or "show" occurs about 20 times in chaps. 40-48; and it is used with special reference to this "future problem" as we may call it: the power of Israel's God to foretell future events and to bring them to pass as foretold, and the utter impotence of the idol-gods to do either the one or the other. Cf. Isa. 19:12.

[4] Cf. 42:9; 43:9-13; 44:7; 45:11, 21f.; 46:8-11; 48:14f.; also 37:26.

[5] They occur especially frequently in chaps. 40-66. "Jehovah" is the usual name for Deity in both parts of Isaiah. It occurs 228 times in chaps. 1-39 and 193 times in chaps. 40-66. Cf. R. D. Wilson, "The Names of God in the O. T." (*Princeton Theol. Rev.*, vol. xviii, pp. 461f.). The title "Jehovah of hosts," which occurs about 40 times in chaps. 1-39 is rare in 40-66 (44:6; 45:13; 47:4; 48:2; 51:15; 54:5). "Holy One of Israel" occurs 21 times in Isa. of which 10 are in chaps. 40-66.

An Arrangement of Isaiah 44:24-28

Exhibiting the Numerico-Climactic Structure of

THE POEM OF THE TRANSCENDENCE OF THE LORD GOD OF ISRAEL

Thus-saith-the-LORD thy-redeemer   and-thy-fashioner from-(the-)womb

I-am the-Lord

that-made all

that-stretched-out heavens alone

that-spread-out the-earth: who(was-)with-me?

that-frustrateth (the-)signs of-liars   and-vaticinators he-maketh-frenzied

that-turneth wise-men backward   and-their-wisdom he-maketh-folly

that-confirmeth the-word of-his-servant   and-the-counsel of-his-messengers he-performeth

that-saith of-Jerusalem she-shall-be-inhabited   and-of-the-cities of-Judah they-shall-be-built   and-their-waste-places I-will-build-up

that-saith to-(the-)Deep: dry-up   and-thy-rivers I-will-dry-up

that-saith of-Cyrus, my-shepherd(-is-he)   and-all my-pleasure shall-be-perform   even-to-say of-Jerusalem she-shall-be-built   and-(of-the-) temple, thy-foundation-shall-be-laid

He that formed thee from the womb." In chapters 43-45 such expressions almost become a refrain. The two descriptive words, "redeemer" and "former" (fashioner), which appear together here, also occur rather frequently in this group of chapters and especially in this context. The special claim of the God of Israel upon His people is that He is their *Redeemer* (41:14).[6] He has redeemed them in the past; and He will do it in the future. The fact that He is the Author of their being is also stressed (43:1);[7] and this is done in direct contrast to the vain works of the idolaters (44:9, 10, 12). For while they can indeed fashion a graven image, a dumb idol, they cannot make it live or move or talk. They are, so to speak, in the "dolly" stage of human existence; and their idol-gods cannot even say, Papa! or Mama! And they themselves are as senseless as the idols which they have made. They know not the God who formed them and created all the things that are (40:28; 42:5; 45:18).

THE PRONOUNCEMENT

This impressive introduction is followed by the even more impressive declaration, "I *am* the LORD." This great affirmation that the One who here speaks to Israel is Jehovah their covenant God runs like a refrain throughout this group of chapters.[8] Less frequent are "I *am* He,"[9] "I *am* God" (43:12; 45:22), and "I *am* thy God" (41:10). Usually it has joined with it one or more descriptive phrases which emphasize the significance of this great declaration: e.g., "I *am* the LORD, the first and with the last, I *am* He" (41:4); "I *am* the LORD thy God, that holdeth thy right hand, that saith to thee, Fear not I will help thee" (41:13); "I *am* the LORD, which sanctifieth thee, the creator of Israel, his king" (43:15).[10]

---

[6] Cf. 41:14; 43:14; 44:6, 24; 47:4; 48:17; 49:7, 26; 54:5, 8; 59:20; 60:16; 63:16. The finite verb also occurs 8 times in these chapters, and the passive participle ("redeemed") 4 times. This root occurs in chaps. 1-39 only in 35:9. Another root with similar meaning is rare in Isa. It occurs in 1:27; 29:22; 35:10; 50:2; 51:11.

[7] "Create" and "form" (fashion) each occur a score of times in chaps. 40-66. The one occurs once in chaps. 1-39 (4:5), the other three times (22:11; 27:11; 30:14).

[8] 41:13; 42:8; 43:3, 15; 44:24; 45:3, 5, 6, 18; 48:17.

[9] 41:4; 43:10, 13; 46:4; 48:12.

[10] The words "I am the LORD" have a long and interesting history. They occur first in Gen. 15:7 as a simple formula of introduction. Compare "I am God almighty" (Gen. 17:1, 35:11); also "I am Pharaoh" (41:44), "I am Joseph" (45:3). This simple formula occurs in Ex. 6:2, 6, 8, 29; and it becomes almost a refrain in Lev. 18-26, where it is used again and again to state the warrant for the laws proclaimed through Moses. It is frequently expanded by adding the words "your" (thy) God" (e.g., Ex. 6:7) and such descriptive clauses as, "which brought thee out of the land of Egypt, out of the house of bondage" (Ex. 20:2).

THE PROOF

In view of the frequence with which this affirmation, "I am the LORD," appears and the variety of forms in which it is used, it is to be noted that nowhere in the entire book of Isaiah and nowhere else in the entire Bible is it used so impressively as here.[11] Nowhere else do we find such an abundance of supporting evidence to show the uniqueness of Him who thus describes Himself. For in this passage the declaration "I am the LORD" is followed by *nine* clauses all of which are intended to declare, describe, and prove the incomparable greatness of Him who bears this mighty and glorious Name. And it is also to be noted that the very fact that they are adduced for the purpose of proving the unique claims of the God of Israel also serves to show their own intrinsic importance. They are some of the "mighty acts" of that transcendent Being who styles Himself, the LORD God of Israel.

In the Hebrew each of these nine clauses begins with a participle which agrees with and modifies the word "LORD." The AV and ARV have rendered all of them by relative clauses beginning with "that." But this should not make it any less obvious to the reader that they all stand in direct relation to and enlarge upon the great affirmation, "I am the LORD." Furthermore, it is to be noted at once that these nine clauses are arranged in a chronological sequence the aim of which is to show that the God of Israel is sovereign in all the affairs of men, that past, present, and future events are all within His control and determined by Him.

A further modification of the formula makes it the object of a clause of purpose "that they (thou, ye) may know that I am the LORD" (Ex. 7:17, 8:18) or express the result, "and ye shall know that I am the LORD" (Ex. 6:7, 7:5). It thus expresses the reason for all God's dealings with His people and with their enemies, both in grace and in chastisement (e.g., 1 Kgs. 20:13, 28). This form is rare in Isa. (45:3, 6; 49:23, 26; 60:10), but in Ezek. it becomes a refrain which occurs some 60 times (cf. Allis, *The Five Books of Moses,* 2nd ed., p. 66).

[11] It is noteworthy how frequently in Isa. 40-66 the personal pronoun "I" is used emphatically of the God of Israel. This is true not only of the expressions just considered; it also occurs a number of times where the pronominal subject of the verb, which as in the case of Latin and Greek is ordinarily simply indicated by the formative ending (or preformative), is expressed by the independent pronoun also. It is also worthy of note that in the formula as it occurs here, "I am the LORD" (44:24), the longer form of the independent pronoun "I" (*anoki*) is used despite the fact that in this expression the shorter form (*ani*) is regularly used. This may be for the sake of emphasis and rhythm, to make this great affirmation, which is to be followed by nine descriptive clauses, as emphatic and conspicuous as possible. The longer form occurs nearly 20 times in chaps. 40-66 and is usually emphatic (e.g., 43:11, 25; 51:12).

NUMBER AND CLIMAX

If the reader will turn to the Arrangement of the poem given in the CHART, he will observe that the nine relative clauses which follow the declaration "I am the LORD" are arranged in three groups or strophes which vary very greatly in length. The first group consists of three simple relative clauses. In the second group, each of the three clauses is expanded by the addition of a clause, which begins with "and" and ends with a finite verb.[12] In the third group, two of these "and clauses," as we may call them, are added in the first line, in the second only one, while in the third there are three, an average of two each for the three lines of the strophe.[13] So we may say that the first strophe consists of three single-member lines, the second of three double-member lines, the third of three lines which average triple-member lines. Hence, we observe at the outset a very remarkable symmetry in the structure of the poem, an arrangement which is clearly climactic; and we observe at the same time a variation especially marked in the third group or strophe which increases the climax at the end very considerably.

In view of the remarkable structure of this prophetic poem, as it has just been briefly described, it is to be carefully noted, before we enter into a detailed discussion of it, that the striking arrangement given it is clearly required by the structure of the passage itself. The arrangement is simply an attempt to present the prophecy to the reader in a form which will make this structure clear. It shows that every one of the nine lines consists of or begins with a relative clause which depends directly on the word "LORD." It also shows that all of the additional clauses or members are added on by means of "and" (or, "even") to the one which precedes and that each of these clauses ends with a finite verb. In order to make this clear the familiar rendering of the AV has been altered to some extent. Besides this, hyphens

---

[12] In the verbal sentence in Hebrew, the verb usually stands at the beginning. But its position may vary considerably; and in poetry or elevated prose we often find it at the end. This may be primarily for emphasis. E.g., "I before thee I will go, and the crooked places I will make straight, the gates of bronze I will break in pieces, and the bars of iron I will cut in sunder" (Isa. 45:2). Sometimes the order is chiastic, the second clause reversing the order of the first. E.g., "I will lay waste mountains and hills, and all their herbs I will dry up; and I will make the rivers islands, and the pools I will dry up" (Isa. 42:15). Here in Isa. 44:24-28 the order may be regarded as emphatic, the unusual order emphasizing both the verb and the object of the verb.

[13] The rendering "even-to-say of-Jerusalem" in the last line of the poem is only an apparent exception to this rule. The same conjunction is used in the Hebrew in all nine cases. It may be rendered both "and" and "even." In the context "even" gives a somewhat smoother rendering.

have been used to join together words which render a single word or word-group in the Hebrew. Thus, "and-their-wisdom he-maketh-folly" constitute only two word-groups in the Hebrew, although there are six words in the English rendering. Attention to this feature will make it clear to the reader that in the second and third strophes which have more than one member to the line, all of the members except the last, i.e., all non-end-members, have three words or word-groups each. E.g., in Strophe II, line 1, "That-frustrateth (the-)signs of-liars" has three word-groups while "and-vaticinators he-maketh-frenzied," which is an end-member has only two. But it is to be noted that these slight changes in translation do not involve the slightest change in the Biblical text of this passage. The aim has been simply to clarify it by exhibiting its distinctive and essential features.

It is evident, then, that this passage is clearly marked by two features, *number* and *climax*. The number is *three*. This shows itself in several ways. The nine relative clauses fall apart into three groups of three, which are clearly distinguished by the fact that the first consists of three single-, the second of three double-, the third of an average of three triple-member lines, while even in the length of the members themselves the number three figures prominently, appearing in all the non-end-members. The element of *climax* appears first in the uniform progress or sequence of one-, two-, and three-member groups, and then in the extraordinary climax of the last line of the last strophe. We may represent this graphically as follows by giving to each member the value of unity.

DIAGRAM I

	1			
Strophe I	1			
	1			
	1	1		
Strophe II	1	1		
	1	1		
	1	1	1	
Strophe III	1	1		
	1	1	1	1

This diagram brings out clearly the marked numerical climax in the last line of the poem. If on the other hand we add up the totals for each of the strophes we arrive at the following:

DIAGRAM II

Strophe I   3
Strophe II   3   3
Strophe III   3   3   3

This diagram makes it clear that the extra climax in the last strophe is secured within the numerical structure of the poem. It gives us the normal climax, which is 3, 6, 9; but it does not indicate that within this numerical structure a shift of members has been made for the purpose of securing an additional and special climax at the close of the poem.

THE EXPLANATION OF THE NUMERICAL STRUCTURE

The prominent role which the number three plays in the structure of this prophetical poem naturally raises the question as to the reason for this remarkable arrangement. As has been already intimated, there is nothing mysterious or mystical in this use of the number three. It is simply the number of the ordinary categories of time (past, present, future) with reference to each of which the sovereign control of the Almighty is so stressed in these chapters. The first strophe deals with the *past*, with God's works of creation. The second strophe describes his *present* or providential dealings, with special reference to current events. As the God of history, He is constantly bringing confusion upon all those who endeavor by unauthorized means to ascertain and control that future which belongs peculiarly to Him. But, far more important than that, He is, by His acts, by the course of history rightly understood, constantly confirming and performing everything that He has announced in the past through the "word of his servant" and the "counsel of his messengers." The third strophe refers definitely to the *future*, to the time of the return of Israel to their land and the restoration of its desolations. Past, present, future,—these are the great categories of time; and this great prophetic utterance proclaims the absolute sovereignty of the God of Israel over all of them.

THE EXPLANATION OF THE CLIMACTIC STRUCTURE

Since the explanation of the prominence of the number three is so clearly to be found in the definitely chronological structure of the poem, it is quite proper to infer that the *climactic* feature which is so strikingly combined with the *numerical* will have a similar explanation; that is, that the element of climax is to be found in the relative importance of these three categories of time in the life of mankind, as they are related to the providential government of God. He is the Eternal, the Timeless. But he deals with His creatures in terms of these categories which He has Himself created. Hence His works of creation, providence, and redemption necessarily and inevitably take place and find expression within these three categories. Such being the case, it becomes obvious that both the normal and the special climax of this chronological poem are to be explained with reference to them.

THE NORMAL CLIMAX

The normal climax appears in the regular or uniform sequence of one-, two-, and three-member lines respectively in the three strophes of the poem. This may be said to represent in general the relative importance of the past, the present, and the future in the living and thinking of mankind. The *past* is important. Its record is replete with memorable events and mighty deeds. It has many important lessons for the present. It has warnings and counsels which the present will ignore at its peril. It gives to the present that wisdom of experience which the present greatly needs, if it is to avoid the blunders and profit by the achievements of the generations that are gone. But the past is gone. We cannot call it back. We cannot relive it. We may try to live down or to build upon its record. But it is gone never to return. It has handed over its portfolio to the present; and the place which knew it shall know it no more.

It is different with the *present.* The present is as much greater than the past as a living dog is better than a dead lion. It is the living time, the time of action, the day of achievement or of failure. It is the "invasion day" of life. Whether it speaks in terms of Africa, or of Sicily and Italy, or of the coasts of Normandy, or of the humdrum monotony of "the daily round and the common task," every day is "the Day" in what we sometimes call the battle of life. And all the vanished yesterdays should serve to remind us of the vast importance for weal or woe of the fleeting moment we call Today. It is the time in which we *live!* And in the events of the present we should be constantly endeavoring to see the hand of God guiding and controlling all human affairs for the accomplishment of His purposes.

But the present is, in a very real sense, only the threshold of the *future,* of that portal over which is written, "the things that are coming and shall come." That they are coming, we know. What they will be and when and how they will come, we cannot tell. We know not what a day or an hour may bring forth. But we do know that the future is crowding in upon us with a steady inexorability which may simply appall us when we pause to think of it. In moments of crisis, the certainty of *a* future and the uncertainty of *the* future has tried men's souls as nothing else could do. The agony of suspense! Suicide is the "escape" of those who cannot, dare not, will not face the uncertainty of the future. Sometimes it is dark and ominous and its thunders sound in our ears like the knell of doom. It was such a future which Isaiah set before Hezekiah on that memorable day when the king of Judah showed the ambassadors of the king of Babylon the greatness of his resources. At other times it is like a glorious sunrise which brightens everything with joy and hope, a future which holds before us things that seem "too good to be true." It is such a glorious prospect, lying in that future which is so mysteriously hidden from the eyes of men, which the prophet sets before God's people in this prophecy as the blessing which He has in store for them, return to their own land and the restoration of its desolations. It is the God who in the beginning created all things, and who in the long course of human history has never failed to establish the word which He has spoken through His servant and to perform the counsel which He has made known through His messengers, who now reveals this glorious prospect as His gracious purpose concerning the people He has chosen, the seed of Abraham His friend.

THE SPECIAL CLIMAX

If we may conclude, then, that what we have called the normal climax in the structure of the poem represents the relative importance of past, present, and future, in the ordinary affairs of life and especially at those times when the future prospect is more than ordinarily ominous or auspicious, it becomes important to consider carefully the additional climax which has been introduced into the poem and influences its structure to a very marked degree.

The most noticeable modification in the poem appears in the last strophe which refers definitely to the future. It consists in the shortening of the second line of the strophe to the extent of a single member, and the increasing of the length of the third line to the same extent. Since this makes the last line about twice the length of the one which precedes it, this feature becomes the most striking element in that progressive climax which characterizes the poem as a whole. The question naturally suggests itself whether this marked variation is intentional or might be indicative of a corruption of the text of the poem.

Can we or should we assume that the third member of the second line has been lost or mistakenly connected with the third line? The answer is two-fold. We cannot hold that the second line has simply lost a member. Were this the case, this strophe would have had originally 10 instead of 9 members; and this would destroy the numerical symmetry of the poem. On the other hand, we cannot hold that the second line has lost its *last* member and that this member has been added to the third line. We cannot do this for the reason that the last member of the second line is an end-member (it has two word-groups, or accents),[14] while all the members of the last line except the fourth are non-end-members (they all have three word-groups or accents). This can only mean that the second line has been intentionally shortened and the third lengthened to the extent of a single (non-end) member. The fact that the second line ends with an end-member proves that to be the end of that line. Similarly the fact that the third line has three three-accent members followed by a two-accent member indicates clearly that it was the intention of the writer that the second line should consist of two members and the third of four. If the last member of the second line had three accents and two members of the third line had only two each, there would be good reason for thinking that the present arrangement is due to a corruption of the text. But we do not find this to be the case. On the contrary the structure of the poem as it lies before us furnishes conclusive proof that it correctly represents the plan intended by the poet himself.

A further proof that the exceptional length of the last line of the poem formed a part of the design of the poet is to be found in the fact that it is prepared for to a considerable extent by special features in the first two strophes. The first strophe, as we have seen, consists of three single-member lines. The total of word-groups or accents is nine, an average of three each for the three lines. But it will be noted that the first line has two accents, the second three, while the third has four. This makes the last line about twice as long as the first, a fact which suggests the situation which is to appear so strikingly in the last line of the last strophe. In this case, the climax is uniform, since the strophe consists of a two-, a three-, and a four-accent line.

When we turn to the second strophe, we observe in the end-

---

[14] The shortening of the end-member of the line which is so marked a feature of the second and third strophes of the poem, is a common feature in poetry (a form of *catalexis*). In Hebrew it is so frequent in the book of Lamentations that this 3 + 2 verse has been called the *Qinah* (lamentation) verse. See Appendix V.

members of the three lines a somewhat similar phenomenon, but one which is slightly more like that of the third strophe. The three non-end-members all have three word-groups each. But there is a noticeable difference in the end-members of this strophe. The first consists simply of a noun and a verb. The second consists of a noun plus a pronoun plus a verb, only two word-groups, as in the first line, but with three elements instead of two. This makes it longer, in a sense, than the first line. Yet on the other hand it is actually slightly shorter as regards the length of the words than the first line. The third consists of two nouns plus a pronoun plus a verb and has three accents instead of two. This makes it, as in the case of the last line of the first strophe, appreciably longer than either of the others. And the extra length of this end-member of the last line of the second strophe, like the extra length of the corresponding line of the first strophe, serves to prepare for the extraordinary extension of the third line of the last strophe. The only difference, though an important one is that while in the first two strophes the variation is confined to the end-members themselves, in the last strophe it goes beyond this and involves a change of position of the members which compose the strophe. All of these features taken together constitute clear indication of intention and design in the construction of the poem.

THE MEANING OF THE SPECIAL CLIMAX

Since the detailed analysis which has just been given may seem artificial and even forced to the reader, it is important to pass on at once to consider the connection between the metrical form of the poem, its numerico-climactic structure, and the theme which it sets forth in such detail. For the best explanation and justification of an elaborate and detailed design in the structure of a poem must be found in the fact that it is intended at every step to express and to stress the theme of the author.

The poem celebrates, as we have seen, the absolute uniqueness of the God of Israel in contrast with the impotent nothingness of all so-called gods. It is introduced by the words: "Thus-saith the-LORD, thy-redeemer and-thy-fashioner from-(the-)womb," thus emphasizing both redemption and providence in God's relation to Israel. Then follows the brief declaration: "I-am the-LORD." And this pronouncement is followed by nine relative clauses, which, as they follow one upon the other give what is intended to be a brief catalogue of the mighty acts of the LORD God of Israel. These nine clauses are divided into three groups and refer to the past, the present, and the future.

The first strophe relates to the past. It is a remote past. It is that past which marks the beginning of time as it is known to man, creation. The first statement is both the shortest and also the most general and comprehensive: "that-made all." It asserts tersely and impressively the absolute monergism of the Speaker. Then follows a more definite statement: "that-stretched-out heavens alone." Here the comprehensiveness of the "all" is replaced by "heavens"; and the word "alone" is added to emphasize the monergism already suggested by the "all." The third line is still more definite: "that-spread-out the-earth." The use of the article, *"the* earth," is noticeable because of its omission with the word "heavens." And, instead of the simple word "alone," we meet here the emphatic and challenging phrase, "Who(was-)with-me?",[15] an invitation to anyone, especially to any of the idols of the heathen, to lay claim to the slightest part in these mighty works of the Creator God of Israel. Thus we note a marked increase in definiteness (all—heavens—the earth), coupled with an increasing emphasis (all—alone—who(was-)with-me?) in the course of the strophe. This great claim that Jehovah alone is God and that all things owe their existence to Him and are ordered and controlled by Him is repeatedly made and stressed in these chapters (especially chaps. 40 and 45).[16] And this tremendous fact is sufficient refutation of the vain and empty boast of Babylon, "I and none beside me" (47:8, 10).

The second strophe concerns God's dealings in providence and in redemption. While it declares what we may call God's fixed policy as regards all events—past, present, and future—its position between a clearly past and an equally clearly future strophe, indicates that it is to be regarded as being concerned especially with the present. It deals particularly with that theme which runs as we have seen like a refrain throughout this entire group of chapters, the impotence of the gods of the heathen to reveal the hidden future and the folly of all human efforts to discover and control it, and, on the other hand, the definite claim and the entire competence of the God of Israel to do both. The first two lines are devoted to the negative side of the picture. The Lord discomfits and confounds all those who profess to be able, and who attempt to disclose that future which belongs to Him

---

[15] We meet this challenging and emphatic "who" very frequently in these chapters. Note especially 40:12, 13, 14, 18, 25, 26. See also, 41:2, 4; 42:19 (*bis*), 23, 24; 43:9, 13; 44:7, 10; 45:21; 46:5; 48:14).

[16] Cf. 40:12-18, 22-26; 43:11; 44:6, 8; 45:5, 6, 14, 21; 46:9; 48:12f. In 45:5-6, 21 four different words are used to emphasize this, three of which are of comparatively rare occurrence.

alone. The "liars" (perhaps better rendered "praters" or "boasters"), who like the modern quacks and charlatans give "signs" which are but idle guesses; the "diviners," whose science of augury is directly connected with idolatry and the worship of false gods; the "wise men" who presume to a wisdom which they do not possess—all alike have been and are constantly being confounded and put to shame. It is possible to regard the second line as both weaker and stronger than the first. The first describes two classes of men, the second only one. Those described in the first line put their trust in signs and portents which indicate recognition on their part of an unseen world and of powers higher than their own. Those who are described in the second are content with a worldly wisdom which they think to be sufficient. But they are all alike helpless in dealing with the unknown future. The contrast, however, and a most impressive one, is not between these two lines but between both of them and the third.

"That-confirmeth the-word of-his-servant and-the-counsel of-his-messengers he-performeth." This positive declaration with which the second strophe closes stands in very sharp contrast to the statements which precede it. It is both emphatic and it is definite. The "his servant" and "his messengers" stand in contrast to the indefinite references to "liars," "vaticinators," "wise men" and show that the honor title of the prophet "man of God" is no empty phrase, but a description of that relationship of peculiar intimacy which the prophet enjoys with his God and which makes him the spokesman of One to whom alone the mysterious future is as an open book.

The use of the pronouns "he" and "his" throughout this strophe is especially noteworthy because in both of the others we find the first person used ("I," "me," and "my"). This change from the first person to the third means that, while in those two strophes the Lord Himself is the speaker, in this middle strophe the prophet is speaking about his God. For it seems proper to infer that by "his servant" the prophet means himself. As a prophet he is a servant of the Lord. So here he speaks in his own name and testifies out of his own knowledge and experience to the fact that God, whose servant he is, not only confounds the idolater and the worldly-wise,[17] but establishes the word of His true servant, even as He does the counsel of all His messengers. This explanation accounts for the change of person in this

---

[17] "Wise" and "wisdom" are usually used in Isaiah in the bad sense, of that human wisdom which is but folly in the sight of God. But 11:2 and 33:6 are exceptions.

strophe. It also serves as a specially appropriate introduction to the predictions which immediately follow in the last and climactic strophe of the poem. The past and the future belong especially and exclusively to God. Of the works of creation, which are the theme of the first strophe, no human being can testify, for no human being witnessed them. Of the hidden future none can testify on his own authority. But of the present, of his own day and age, the prophet may be permitted to speak as it were in his own name and on his own authority and to declare as a fact of his own observation and experience, a fact which no one can successfully deny, that the word which the God of Israel places on the lips of His servant must surely come to pass.

What is this "word" which the prophet is so certain that the LORD will "confirm"? While the prophet is in a sense only stating a general principle the truth of which has been demonstrated again and again in the course of God's dealings with His people, it is quite obvious that there is particular reference here to that *word* which forms the third and climactic strophe of the poem, every line of which begins with "that saith." This word concerns the future, the future of an Israel in exile. The first line of the strophe, "that-saith of-Jerusalem, she-shall-be-inhabited, and-of-the-cities of-Judah, they-shall-be-built, and-their-waste-places I-will-build-up," gives what we may call the normal or general scope and perspective of this future strophe, which is the restoration and re-peopling of the land of Judah. When this will take place is not indicated. But it is clearly future. For the strophe deals exclusively with the future: and the fact that the first strophe refers to the remote past, the most remote past of which man has any knowledge or can form any conception, at least suggests, even if it does not definitely prove, that the future which is here described is not immediately impending but rather that it may be decidedly remote, so remote that any disclosure with regard to it will be a signal proof of the unique prerogative of the God of Israel to disclose what lies wholly within His sovereign control. In other words, the return and restoration of which the prophet speaks will follow the period of Israel's desolation and banishment to which chap. 39:6 points forward. Neither of these is present to the mind of the prophet. Both belong to the future.

The second line of this strophe is, as we have seen, noticeably shorter than either of the others. It has only two members, while the first has three and the last has four. This is paralleled by the vagueness and indefiniteness of its contents: "That-saith to-(the-)Deep: dry-up, and-thy-rivers I-will-dry-up." It has been thought by many Bible students that there is a reference here to the diverting of the course of the Euphrates by Cyrus, a stratagem which is mentioned by Herodotus and by Xenophon. But it is more probable that these words contain a general reference to the restoration from Babylon in terms of the Exodus from Egypt, the conspicuous miracle of which was the "drying-up" of the Red Sea (42:15; 43:16; 50:2; 51:10).[18] This interpretation is favored by the claim of Cyrus that Babylon fell to his armies "without battle and conflict."[19] If this interpretation is correct, we have in this line of the strophe an indefinite and figurative statement which is markedly different from the definite and strictly literal statements which precede and follow it. So understood, the contents of this line are in full accord with the structural form of the poem.

The last line of the strophe is the longest: "that-saith of-Cyrus, my-shepherd(-is-he) and-all my-pleasure shall-he-perform, even-to-say of-Jerusalem she-shall-be-built and-(of-the-)temple, thy-foundation-shall-be-laid." This line differs from the second in being entirely literal and very definite. It refers again to the restoration of Jerusalem, as the most important of the desolated cities of Judah, and instead of repeating the promise regarding them, it substitutes the declaration that the temple shall be restored, a promise which however momentous in itself might be regarded as involved or implied in the restoration of the city of which it was the peculiar glory. To this extent the last line is largely a repetition of the predictions of the first line of the strophe. The element of climax consists in the fact that here the prediction of the first line is connected with the name of the person who shall fulfill it, Cyrus, and that the God of Israel gives him the exalted title "my shepherd," declares him to be the one who shall perform "all my pleasure," and proceeds to define this "pleasure" largely in terms of the promises already stated at the beginning of the strophe. Clearly it is the naming of Cyrus, the exalted title which is given him, and the declaration that as the plenipotentiary of the God of Israel he will perform a mighty act of deliverance for His people, which is

---

[18] The fact that this view was favored by Alexander, before the discovery of the Cyrus Cylinder, is one of many examples of the sagacity and caution of that great Biblical scholar.

[19] It is not at all improbable that while the city surrendered to Cyrus' armies without striking a blow, the citadel where Belshazzar was holding high revel was taken by assault (cf. Dan. 6). Sidney Smith (*Isa. xl-lv*, p. 152) finds in the language of the *Cylinder* evidence to show that there was a siege, which resulted in destruction and famine.

responsible for the striking climax in this last line of the poem, a climax which is carefully prepared for throughout the entire structure of the poem.[20] But for this the last line would be little if any advance over the first.

In view of this remarkably close correspondence between the subject-matter of the poem and its literary form, is it not obvious that the striking arrangement of the poem is wholly determined by the requirements of the theme, "the transcendence of Jehovah," and its development along the lines which are so clearly indicated? And is not the fact that this arrangement of the poem does not require the slightest change in its text, not the change or addition or omission of a single word or letter, a striking confirmation of the correctness of the arrangement proposed? An arrangement which was forced and arbitrary would certainly not serve to bring out and emphasize so perfectly the significant features of the poem.

THE DATE OF THE POEM

In view of the oft repeated claim of the critics that the mention of Cyrus by name in 44:28f. and the way he is referred to elsewhere in chaps. 40-48, proves that these prophecies must have been uttered toward the close of the exile, it is a question of great importance whether the remarkable structure which we have observed in the Poem lends support to their contention that it is exilic and therefore not the word of Isaiah the son of Amoz. The answer to this question has already been indicated rather clearly, we think, in the discussion of the poem which has just been completed. But let us look at it again briefly with particular reference to the question of the date.

We have seen that the prophet (1) has constructed his poem according to a definite chronological scheme, with the three logical divisions of past, present, and future clearly indicated; (2) that he has used this number (three) to develop a progressive climax, by gradually increasing the length of the three strophes from one to three members; (3) that he has added to the normal climax a special climax which culminates in the last line of the last strophe and makes it particularly emphatic. We have seen that (4) he makes the first strophe refer exclusively to the remote past, thereby suggesting that the third strophe deals with a distant future; that

---

[20] According to Orelli, "the Persian conqueror is spoken of as a well-known hero of the day, whom one need not mention by name to be understood in alluding to him (xli. 2 ff., 25); only afterwards is his name mentioned, as it were casually (xliv. 28); or this king is addressed as one who has already appeared (xlv. 1)" (*The Prophecies of Isaiah*, p. 212). If Orelli had recognized and understood the structure of the poem, he would not have used the word "casually."

(5) he distinguishes the middle or present strophe from the other
two by a change in person, allowing himself to testify personally
to God's fixed policy regarding future events, viz., that (a) He
baffles every effort of man, whether by recourse to divination or
by the employment of human wisdom, to penetrate the future
and discover its mysteries, and (b) that He unfailingly establishes the word of His true servants concerning it; that (6)
the *word* to which he particularly refers as sure of accomplishment is stated in the three "that saith"s of the future strophe
and concerns the restoration of Israel and Cyrus's connection
with it; and finally (7) that the mention of Cyrus by name in
the last line of this strophe is clearly a climax of definiteness
and supplies the reason for the remarkable construction of the
poem. We submit that if it was the aim of the prophet to
represent Cyrus as belonging to a distant future and the mention
of his name as highly significant and memorable for that very
reason, he has accomplished his task with consummate skill.

We also hold it to be equally clear that, if it had been the aim
of the poet to represent the desolations of Israel as already
taken place, the exile as nearly ended, and Cyrus as already
present, an invincible warrior on the point of attacking Babylon,
the structure of the poem is ill-calculated, to say the least, to
bring out and emphasize these important matters. For it places
Cyrus, who belongs, we are told, to the present and immediate
future—immediacy is stressed by the critics—in the distant
future and gives his mighty deeds an entirely different setting
from the one which the critics hold to be the correct one. Consequently, it is not surprising, in fact it was only to be expected,
that those who regard the words of this poem as the utterance of
a contemporary of Cyrus, should either ignore or fail to recognize the numerico-climactic structure of the poem, despite the
fact that it is so clearly indicated, and should endeavor to give
to it an entirely different form. The arrangement which they
prefer makes of vv. 24-28 a poem of ten lines which is composed
of two stanzas of five lines each (vv. 24-25, 26-28), and each
line of which has two members (the so-called *Qinah* or Pentameter verse). The three main objections to this arrangement
are: that it destroys the symmetrical climax of the poem, that
it cannot be carried through without mutilating the text, and
that the places where it must be assumed that the text is corrupt
are exactly the places where those who attempt to change the
climactic arrangement into the uniform *Qinah* form would be
sure to encounter difficulty in bringing this about.[21]

[21] Cf. Appendix V.

We conclude, therefore, that the claim that Cyrus is referred to in a way which requires us to see in him the contemporary of the prophet is not supported by, but is in direct conflict with, the entire structure and argument of the poem, which aims to make it clear that Cyrus belongs to a distant future. If this be so, the mention of Cyrus by name ceases to be an argument against the unity of Isaiah but becomes instead an argument in favor of it.

In claiming that the Cyrus Poem indicates clearly that Cyrus belongs to the future, we are not unmindful of the fact that in most of the passages which refer to him, he is described with a vividness which suggests that he is already present to the mind of the prophet. This we hold to be quite consistent with, indeed to be an example of, that feature of prophecy to which attention has been already directed and of which other examples will shortly be given, the tendency to represent future events as present or already past. But we hold that here in the Cyrus Poem, in view of the remarkable definiteness and vividness with which Cyrus is introduced, the Spirit of prophecy deemed it needful to make clear that the coming of this mighty deliverer belonged to a distant future.

CHAPTER VI

THE SERVANT OF THE LORD

We turn now to the second and far more important question which is involved in the problem of the unity of the Book of Isaiah, the great figure of the Servant of the Lord, which appears so prominently in chapters 40-66.

These two problems are vitally connected, yet also in a sense quite distinct. In the case of Cyrus there is no question of identity involved. Scarcely any one denies that the Cyrus referred to is Cyrus the Great, the conqueror of Babylon. The great question has been, as we have seen, whether Cyrus is referred to as belonging to the distant future or as a contemporary of the prophet. In the case of the Servant on the contrary the question of identity is the main problem; and acceptance of the "contemporary" theory of prophecy as applied to Cyrus has made the identifying of the Servant a vexing and difficult one for the critics. In fact the interpretation of the Servant passages in Isaiah has been for some years the most vigorously debated problem in connection with the Book of Isaiah.[1]

As has been intimated above, there are remarkable and significant points of resemblance in the way in which these two prominent figures, Cyrus and the Servant, are brought before us. The most important are these:

(1) As in the case of Cyrus, the Servant is a *frequently occurring* figure in these chapters. In fact the references to the Servant are even more widely scattered than those which refer to Cyrus. The first passage is 41:8 and the last is 53:11f.[2] Four of these passages are often called the "Songs of the Servant"

[1] One of the most recent discussions of this subject is the monograph by C. R. North, *The Suffering Servant in Deutero-Isaiah, an Historical and Critical Study* (1948). The thoroughness of the discussion is indicated by the fact that the "list of works consulted" covers more than 12 pages, or approximately 250-300 works. The viewpoint of the author is "critical" as is made clear in the title of the book; and he points out that recent defenders of the conservative position have been in the main Roman Catholics. Among these one of the more recent is J. S. van der Ploeg (*Les Chants du Serviteur de Jahvé*, 1936).

[2] "Servant" occurs 20 times in Isaiah 40-53. The servant is called "Israel" (49:3), Jacob (48:20), "Jacob Israel" (41:8, 9; 44:1, 2, 21; 45:4). He is called "my servant" (42:1, 19 [cf. 44:21]; 43:10; 49:6; 52:13; 53:11). "His servant" (44:26; 49:5; 50:10) "a servant of rulers" (49:7). In 44:2 the epithet "Jeshurun" is added, and in 53:11, the word "righteous." It is worthy of note that while the word "servant" also appears 11 times in chaps. 54-66, it is always in the plural (54:17; 56:6; 63:17; 65:8-9, 13 (*ter*), 14-15; 66:14). Since the division of 40-66 into 40:55, 56-66 is so popular today, it is interesting to note that the use of the plural begins in chap. 54.

81

(42:1-4; 49:1-6; 50:4-9; 52:13-53:12); and 61:1-3 should certainly be included among them, despite the fact that the word "servant" does not occur in it.[3]

(2) We observe in the case of the Servant, the same *vividness* of portrayal which we have found to be characteristic of the Cyrus passages. The Servant is represented as present in the thought of the prophet. He is spoken *of;* he is spoken *to;* and he even speaks *himself.* In 42:1-4 the Lord says of him, "Behold my servant whom I uphold . . . I have put my spirit upon him." This means that he is prepared and equipped for his task and the rest of the passage describes its nature. In 49:1-6, the servant himself speaks and calls on all men to attend to his words: "The LORD hath called me from the womb"; and the whole description is in the past tense or the present. Note especially v. 4, "But I said I have labored in vain and spent my strength in vain." The Servant speaks again in 50:4-9 and here also the perfect tense is used repeatedly: "I gave my back to the smiters . . . I did not hide my face from insult and from spitting." In 52:13-53:12 in which the sufferings of the Servant are most fully and graphically described we find that the description is, in so far as the sufferings themselves are concerned, entirely in the past tense.[4] This applies also to 61:1-3 in which the Servant declares that "the LORD hath anointed me to preach glad tidings . . . he hath sent me to bind up the brokenhearted." This means that the One of whom the prophet speaks in these "Songs" is so clearly present to his thought that he can describe his mission as being fulfilled before his very eyes, or even as already fulfilled, and that he can even introduce the Servant as Himself speaking and declaring his mission and the equipment He has received for accomplishing it. In other words the Servant is just as much present to the eye of the prophet in these passages as Cyrus is in those which describe him, with the exception of the poem which has just been discussed.

---

[3] As to the question whether 61:1-3 should be included among the "Songs," G. A. Smith in 1890 regarded the evidence as "not conclusive" (*Bk of Isaiah* ii. 435). But Duhm's insistence that Trito-Isaiah begins with 56:1 has led many critics to conclude that 61:1-3 should be regarded as distinct from the Servant Songs.

It is unfortunate that in v. 2 the A.V. has the rendering, "For he shall grow up before him." The correct rendering is, "and he grew up before him" (cf. RV) The imperfect tense in v. 10 "when (or, if) his soul shall make an offering for sin" (RV) indicates that as Alexander points out we have here the beginning of the "exaltation" which the prophet consistently describes as future. Cf. Heb. 9:12, 24f. The entrance into heaven was first of all the presentation before the Father in the holy place not made with hands the evidence of His full atonement for sin; by "his own blood" (9:12) he entered as High Priest into heaven itself and is now seated at the right hand of the Father.

(3) The *complexity* or two-sidedness which we have noted in the Cyrus Prophecies is even more marked in those which describe the Servant. He is called "Israel" and "Jacob" (e.g., 41:8). He is deaf and blind (42:18f.), sinful and in need of redemption (44:22, cf. 43:25). Yet he is also pictured as one who has a mission to Israel and the Gentiles (42:1-7, 49:1-6), as one who has suffered grievous cruelty, though he has not been rebellious but has trusted in the Lord (50:6-9), as one who has suffered uncomplainingly, not for his own sins, but for the sins of others (53:4-6), as one who will be gloriously vindicated and greatly honored in days to come (52:13-15; 53:10b-12). These contrasted and even sharply conflicting representations have occasioned expositors much difficulty. There are, broadly speaking, two ways of explaining them: difference in authorship and difference in theme.

Many of those who date chaps. 40-55 near the close of the Exile, maintain that the four Songs of the Servant are later insertions in this group of chapters. Their main argument for this position is that the representation of the Servant is so different in them that they cannot have the same subject or be by the same writer as the rest of 40-55; and they have sought to strengthen it by the claim that these Songs show little or no connection with the contexts in which they stand, and also that there is a similarity between the four songs themselves which points to the same author for all or most of them. On the other hand those who regard the "Songs" as by the same author as the rest of Isa. 40-55 account for the difference as due to a change in the viewpoint or theme of the prophet himself. At first the prophet was convinced, and expressed his conviction and earnest hope with great positiveness, that Cyrus would declare himself to be the Lord's Servant. But when Cyrus attributed his triumph over Babylon to Bel and Nebo instead of to Jehovah, then according to this theory, the prophet set forth in the Songs that conception of the true Servant which Cyrus had so sadly failed to realize.

The other and older solution is that given, for example by Alexander and by Delitzsch.[5] Accepting the unity of authorship

[5] Delitzsch steadfastly maintained the unity of chaps. 40-66. He recognized three groups, each of which had a 3 x 3 structure, an analysis corresponding in general with the 27 chapters of the A.V. He never fully accepted the critical theory of more than one Isaiah. In the third edition of his *Commentary* (1879), he maintained the unity of authorship, but insisted that, as far as exegesis was concerned, the question of a Deutero-Isaiah was immaterial, since the author of chaps. 40-66 wrote as one living in the time of exile (p. 411). Consequently, the phrase, "the Deutero-Isaianic book of consolation" in his *Messianic Prophecies* (translated from a student's lecture notes by S. J. Curtis in 1880, p. 87) is misleading because ambiguous. Delitzsch always maintained that Isaiah might have written the entire book; and he never gave unqualified approval to the theory of a Deutero-Isaiah. Cf. E. J. Young (*op. cit.*, vol. ix., pp. 21-24).

of these chapters, they explained the differences in representation as due to the diversity-in-unity of the subject described. The subject of all the Servant Passages is Israel. The three aspects of the subject dealt with are: sinful Israel, pious Israel, and that "Israelite indeed in whom is no guile," who was declared to be "the Son of God with power by the resurrection from the dead." Using the familiar NT figure of the Head and the Body, Alexander stated the solution as follows:

> "If it be asked, how the different applications of this honorable title [Israel] are to be distinguished so as to avoid confusion or capricious inconsistency, the answer is as follows. Where the terms are in their nature applicable both to Christ as the Head and to his Church as the Body, there is no need of distinguishing at all between them. Where sinful imperfection is implied in what is said, it must of course apply to the body only. Where a freedom from such imperfection is implied, the language can have a direct and literal reference only to the Head, but may be considered as descriptive of the body, in so far as its idea or design is concerned, though not in its actual condition. Lastly, when any thing is said implying deity or infinite merit, the application to the Head becomes not only predominant but exclusive."[6]

Delitzsch has drawn the same distinctions, but has illustrated them by the use of a different figure, the pyramid. "The lowest part," he tells us, "is all-Israel, the middle section the Israel which is not according to the flesh but according to the spirit, the Apex is the Person of the Mediator of salvation who arises out of Israel."[7] This interpretation, whichever figure is used to illustrate it, serves to bring out very clearly the vital connection and the marked and vastly important differences which mark the figure of the Servant as drawn for us in the Second Part of Isaiah. This interpretation has consequently this advantage over the solution offered by the critics, in that it seeks to do justice to both the resemblances and the differences, while the tendency with those who allege diversity of authorship is to stress the differences in order to justify their solution of them.

In view of the widely different meanings which must be given to the word "servant," it is to be noted that the four "Songs" include only passages which belong in the second and third of the classifications proposed by Alexander and Delitzsch: "spiritual Israel" and "the Mediator of salvation who arises out of Israel." Thus in 49:1-9 we have a reference to that spiritual Israel, which both together with and also in the Person of her exalted Head is to bring salvation to Israel and to the Gentiles

---

[6] Alexander, *op. cit.*, ii., p. 50.

[7] Delitzsch, *Jesaia* (1879), p. 439. Urwick (*The Servant of Jehovah*, 1877, p 94) uses the figure of concentric circles with the Messiah at the center.

(cf. Acts 13:47). On the other hand in chap. 53 we have, using Alexander's figure, an application to the Head which is both "predominant and exclusive." In the further discussion we shall confine ourselves largely, though not exclusively, to the interpretation of Isaiah 53. But before we do this another important matter is still to be considered.

An Important Difference Between the Cyrus and the Servant Passages

We have been considering the interesting and significant resemblances between these two groups of passages in Isaiah 40-66: the frequency of their occurrence, the vividness of the portrayal, and the complexity of the representation. It remains for us to note a difference which is of great importance and requires very careful consideration.

In a very real sense the problem of Cyrus is an Old Testament problem, we might even say, merely and exclusively an Old Testament problem. Cyrus is never mentioned in the New Testament. His career is, at least in outline, fairly well-known to us. Herodotus, the historian, wrote about him in the age of Pericles, a century after his death. He soon became an almost legendary figure. Xenophon made him the hero of his *Cyropaedia*, Cicero refers to him in *De Senectute* in a way which shows that his memory was still green in his day. And the spade of the archaeologist has within a few decades unearthed a cylinder which gives us a contemporary account of his conquest of Babylon. But Cyrus belongs to the distant past. Five hundred years lie between him and the Augustan Age. We may see in him a type of the Messiah. For he freed Israel from a grievous bondage which was the penalty and punishment of sin. But he was only a type. And when the titles, "shepherd" and "anointed," are viewed in the light of the words, "though thou hast not known me," they make poignantly clear the fact that Cyrus, great and noble-spirited monarch though he may have been, was only a feeble and heathen type of Israel's true Messiah who is the Saviour of Israel and the world.

On the other hand, it is of the greatest importance to remember that the Servant of the Lord is very definitely a New Testament figure. Thus in Matt. 12:15-21, Jesus' withdrawal from the multitudes is justified by the quoting of Isa. 42:1-3, the quotation being introduced by the words: "That it might be fulfilled which was spoken by Esaias the prophet saying." Chap. 49:1-6 is appealed to in Acts 13:47 (cf. Lk. 2:31f.) as finding its ful-

fillment in the proclamation of the Gospel by the apostles of
the Lord. Note the words which introduce the quotation: "for
so hath the Lord commanded us." We are told that, when the
book of the prophet Esaias was given to him in the synagogue
at Nazareth, Jesus found the place where it was written, "The
Spirit of the Lord is upon me" (Isa. 61:1f.) and when He had
read it He said, "This day is this scripture fulfilled in your ears"
(Lk. 4:17-21). Isa. 53:1 is quoted in whole or part in Jn. 12:38
and Rom. 10:16 as fulfilled in the refusal of the Jews to receive
Jesus as the Christ and to accept the Gospel as preached by his
ambassadors. Verse 4 is quoted in part as fulfilled in Jesus'
ministry of healing (Mt. 8:17). Verses 5-6 contain phrases
which are used in 1 Pet. 2:24f. Verses 7-8 are quoted in Acts
8:32f. and referred to Jesus by Philip the evangelist. Verse 9
is clearly referred to in 1 Pet. 2:22. Verse 12 is quoted in part in
Lk. 22:37 (cf. Heb. 9:28). These New Testament passages con-
front us with an important question which does not concern us
in the case of Cyrus.

CHAPTER VII

WHO IS THE SUFFERING SERVANT OF ISAIAH 53?

This question, which has become especially acute today in view of the popularity of the critical interpretation of prophecy, is not a new one. As we have just seen it was raised very early in the history of the Christian Church. When Philip met the Ethiopian eunuch, as he was engaged in the reading of "Isaiah the prophet," and asked him the pertinent, yet rather impertinent-sounding question, "Understandest thou what thou readest?", he was met at once with the confession, "How can I except some one should guide me?" And when Philip accepted the eunuch's invitation to sit with him in his chariot, the question which was put to him regarding the words of 53:7f. was this, "I pray thee, of whom speaketh the prophet this? of himself, or of some other?" This was the question which naturally suggested itself to the eunuch and with which he felt unable to cope. This was the difficult question which he placed before Philip. It is a vitally important question; and it is one the answer to which has divided the Jew and the Unitarian from the Evangelical Christian throughout the centuries. It is a difficult and intricate question, as some regard it. But it does not seem to have caused Philip either dismay or confusion. We are simply told that Philip "beginning from this scripture, preached unto him Jesus." As a result of this preaching the eunuch was baptized. This means that according to the New Testament, the suffering Servant of the Old Testament is a New Testament figure. The words of the prophet have their fulfilment in Jesus the Christ. This is the important difference between the prophecies regarding Cyrus and those which concern the Servant, aside of course from the immeasurable difference which separates them in other respects. Such being the case, when we come to compare these two groups of prophecies and to estimate them in terms of the two criteria which as we have seen figure so largely in the present controversy as to the *nature* and *meaning*, the *situation* and *scope* of prophecy, there are we believe only two thoroughly consistent methods of interpretation.

The Traditional Interpretation

According to this view, which rests upon the acceptance of the well-founded and, until recently generally accepted, tradition that the entire Book of Isaiah comes to us from the pen of the great prophet of the Assyrian period, Isaiah the son of Amoz. the problem of Cyrus and the problem of the Suffering Servant of chap. 53 are essentially the same. Both refer to the distant future, to a future which in both cases is far too remote for the unaided vision of the wisest of men to penetrate its mysteries. In the one case the interval is proved by the course of events to be more than a century, in the other it is more than seven centuries. But while this may make the element of foresight and prediction greater in the one case than in the other, there is no essential difference between them. Both deal with events lying far beyond the contemporary scene in which the prophet and his hearers are living their busy and eventful lives. In their *scope* both prophecies refer not to the present, not to the immediate future, but to non-existent situations, to events which only the eyes of future generations will behold and marvel at.

As regards the other aspect of prophecy which is so stressed in the modern critical interpretation, the matter of *situation*, these prophecies are as we have seen strikingly similar. Both speak of an individual and describe his career with a vividness and circumstantiality which seems to make the speaker an eyewitness of the events which he describes. In the case of the Suffering Servant the prophet writes as one who has witnessed the awful tragedy of Calvary, and who looks forward with confidence to the glory which will surely follow. In the case of Cyrus, while as we have seen he indicates quite clearly that Cyrus belongs to the distant future, he nevertheless usually speaks of him as one who has already entered upon that career which is to have such tremendous significance for God's people who will then be bearing the yoke of captivity in a foreign land. Consequently, the traditional interpretation may well claim to be a logical and consistent one. Once the theory of prophecy which we have seen to be consistently taught in Scripture is admitted, there are no serious difficulties connected with the interpretation of these prophecies. In saying this we do not mean to assert that all is clear and obvious, that there are no obscure and difficult passages, but simply that, on the basis of a system of interpretation which recognizes predictive prophecy as a fact, an obviously supernatural fact, those who accept the Messianic interpretation of Isaiah 53 on the authority of the New Testament will, or at least need, have no real difficulty in believing that the prophet who foretold the sufferings of Christ in chap. 53 could also foretell the coming of Cyrus many centuries before that vastly greater event. Or, to state the issue negatively, it is this: "Deny to Isaiah the son of Amoz the prediction concerning Cyrus, and it is but logical to go farther and deny to him the Messianic hope which is usually associated with his name."[1] That such is the case will become unmistakably plain, we believe, when the critical interpretations of Isaiah 53 are carefully examined.

THE CRITICAL INTERPRETATIONS

These interpretations have broadly speaking two forms which we may call, for want of a better principle of differentiation, the *consistent* and the *inconsistent* critical interpretations.

The Consistent Critical Interpretation. If it is insisted that the prophecies regarding Cyrus must be dated shortly before the fall of Babylon because Cyrus is described as one already well-known as a conqueror, and as being on the point of striking at Babylon, then there are only two consistent views which can be held with regard to the subject of Isa. 53, whose sufferings are just as vividly present to the mind of the prophet as the critics hold to be the case with Cyrus, the deliverer, and his victorious career. There are just two situations to which the consistent critic can assign the prophecy.

(a) If the prophecy is regarded as Messianic, then it must have been uttered by one who was either an actual witness of the Crucifixion, or who knew and spoke of it as an accomplished fact, and who also looked forward with joyous confidence to the glorious results which would follow the sufferings of the Saviour. These two features are especially significant. Not only are the sufferings on the Cross represented as already accomplished: "Surely he hath borne our griefs, and carried our sorrows," so that we hear, as it were, the words "It is finished," fall from the lips of the dying Saviour; but this fact, that the sufferings are finished, is made all the more conspicuous and noteworthy because these sufferings are set in the *framework* of the glory which is to follow them. Isaiah 52:13 begins with the words, "Behold, my servant shall deal prudently, he shall be exalted and shall be extolled, and shall be very high." Delitzsch declares that we have here "the beginning, the progress, and the culmination or summit of the exaltation" of Christ;[2] and he adds, "Stier is not wrong when he reminds us of the Resurrection, Ascension, and Session at God's right hand, the three main steps in the fulfilment in history of the *exaltatio*." Similary at the close (53:10*b*-12) the description is in terms of the future: "He shall see of the

---

[1] G. L. Robinson, *op. cit.*, p. 1508.

[2] Delitzsch, *op. cit.*, p. 535.

travail of his soul, and shall be satisfied." Thus, the humiliation of the Cross, as a great achievement that has been fully and finally accomplished, is set in a glorious framework, surrounded by the glory which shall follow it as by a golden halo. The contrast between what the Servant *has* done is made all the more conspicuous by the emphasis which is placed on the glorious rewards which the Servant is yet to receive as a recompense for the sufferings which he has already endured.

It is perfectly obvious, of course, that chap. 53 cannot have been uttered by one who was actually a witness of the death of Christ. Some of the most radical of the critics, it is true, have dated large portions of Isaiah, including chap. 53, as late as the 2nd century B.C., or even the beginning of the 1st century for the completion of the entire work. But that is as far as they have ventured to go.[3] Aside from all other considerations even so late a date as the second century is rendered highly precarious by the fact that the LXX version, which contains the whole of Isaiah was probably made in the 2nd century B.C., if not earlier; and if the recently discovered Isaiah Scroll dates from as early as the middle of that century, such extreme views must be admitted by the critics themselves to be untenable. Whenever penned, Isaiah 53 was not written by an actual eyewitness of the Crucifixion. So if the prophet must be speaking of a contemporary, the Messianic solution is definitely eliminated. The prophet can not be speaking of the sufferings of Christ.

(b) If, on the other hand, the stress is laid on the *situation* of the Prophet a quite different conclusion is indicated. If the date is approximately the close of the Babylonian Captivity, then in speaking of the Servant the Prophet must have in mind some historical personage cf his own day; e.g., Jehoiachin, Zerubbabel, Cyrus, Sheshbazzar, Meshullam. Or he may be thinking of some historical figure of the past, whether the recent past, e.g. of Uzziah, Hezekiah, Josiah, Jeremiah or Ezekiel, or of some more remote figure, such as Moses or Job. Such a view is required by the fact that the sufferings are described as *past*. Some fifteen identifications with names which figured more or less prominently in Old Testament history have been suggested. But no one of them has gained wide or lasting acceptance with the critics.

Closely related to these attempts to discover the person of the sufferer in a historical individual of Old Testament times is the

---

[3] Notably R. H. Kennett, who in his Schweich Lectures of 1909 assigned 33 whole chapters (14 of which were in the First Part) and portions of 13 others to the 2nd cty. B.C. Kennett admitted that much ancient material might be included in these passages. But in their present form he assigned them to this late date.

proposal to discover him in the prophet himself. This autobiographical interpretation was proposed about thirty years ago. But aside from the fact that it identifies the sufferer with a prophet who is himself utterly unknown, there is the added objection that the prophet could not have described his own death. So it becomes necessary to assume that chap. 53 is a lament or elegy composed by the prophet's followers after his death, in which they confess their failure to understand and appreciate their master.[4]

Other scholars have had recourse to less definite identifications. It has been suggested that the sufferer represents the line of the prophets (cf. Acts 7:52), or of the priests. Some have had recourse to a mythological interpretation attempting to find in the Suffering Servant a form or echo of the ritual myth of the dying and reviving god (Tammuz-Adonis, or Bel-Marduk).[5]

Probably the majority of those who hold the critical theory have seen in the Servant of the "Songs," a *personification of Israel*,[6] either the whole nation suffering in exile at the hands of and for the sake of the nations, or a pious remnant in Israel, a remnant misunderstood and persecuted by the nation as a whole, but suffering for the sins of Israel and of the nations. There is also much difference of opinion as to whether this personification is collective or individual, real or ideal.[7]

There are two main objections to this view that the Sufferer is a contemporary of the prophet, whether an actual person or an ideal figure or personification.

The first is the obvious fact that the Sufferer is clearly represented as a substitutionary sacrifice, as one who, himself sinless, suffers for the sins of others. This is made particularly clear in

[4] This interpretation was proposed by Mowinckel in 1921. North regarded the publication of Mowinckel's monograph (*Der Knecht Jahwäs*) as sufficiently important to mark the end of the second of the three periods into which he has divided the history of the "modern" interpretation of Isa. 53. He entitles it "From Duhm to Mowinckel." But he points out that Mowinckel later rejected this theory and that it is not as popular now as when first proposed. Cf. North, *op. cit.*, pp. 72-85; also van der Ploeg, *Les Chants du Serviteur de Jahvé*, pp. 125-135.

[5] Discussed by Sidney Smith, *op. cit.*, pp. 17f., 101f.

[6] Moffatt did not hesitate to introduce this interpretation into the *text* of his Version of the O. T. He did this by changing the "shall deal prudently" (*yaskil*) of 52:13 into "Israel" (*Yisra'el*), rendering "Behold, my servant Israel, yet shall raise." There is no objective warrant for this; the similarity of the words does not justify it. He also inserted "Israel" as the subject of the first verb of 53:2, "Why, Israel of old grew like a sapling." He made these changes without any hint to the reader that this was not the rendering of the Hebrew text!

[7] North (*op. cit.*, p. 200) quotes Skinner as holding that the main question at issue is not between collective and individual theories but between *historical* and *ideal*.

vv. 6-7. Of this passage Alexander has truly said, "If vicarious suffering can be described in words, it is so described in these two verses."[8] It was "our sins" that He bore. It was for "our transgressions" that He was wounded. These and similar statements in this wonderful chapter become especially significant when we study them in the light of the situation out of which the critics believe that this remarkable description arose.

In marked contrast to the descent into Egypt, the destruction of Jerusalem and the Babylonian Captivity are definitely declared to be the punishment for sin, the sin of the nation and of the individual. Jeremiah declares that, "if ye can find a man, if there be *any* that executeth judgment," (5:1), the Lord will pardon the city. Elsewhere he tells us: "Though Moses and Samuel stood before me, yet my mind could not be toward this people" (15:1). Moses had interceded successfully for Israel at Sinai, when they turned aside and "made the calf which Aaron made" (Ex. 32:7-14). Samuel had prayed for Israel at Mizpeh and the Lord gave them the Ebenezer victory (1 Sam. 7). But now no such intercession, however powerful could avail. Even more pointedly Ezekiel declares that were there in the wicked city of Jerusalem men so conspicuous for piety as Noah, Daniel, and Job, they would be able to save but "their own selves by their righteousness"; they should save "neither son nor daughter" (14:14, 20). These words which come to us from two great prophets of the exilic period declare with the utmost plainness the meaning of the Captivity which Israel was to endure and did endure for seventy long years. They reject emphatically the idea that Israel was suffering unmerited punishment for the sake of the heathen nations. They reject still more plainly the idea of a "pious remnant" in Israel suffering for the sins of the nation as a whole and the sins of the Gentiles as well.[9] On the contrary they indicate with the utmost clearness that the One of whom it is said that He "bare the sin of many," that on him was laid "the iniquity of us all," that "for the transgression of my people he was smitten," cannot be any Israelite of the past or present, cannot be Israel or the pious remnant of Israel. Yet the consistent

---

[8] Alexander, *op. cit.*, vol. ii., p. 264.

[9] According to Jeremiah, the pious remnant were the "good figs" who were carried captive to Babylon for "good" (chap. 24), that they might be spared the horrors of sword, famine and pestilence which the Lord was bringing upon the evil generation of Israel. They were the "Noah, Daniel, and Job" who saved only "their own selves by their righteousness."

advocates of the critical theory of prophecy have been endeavoring for decades to establish such an identification, to find some individual, some group of individuals, belonging to the Old Testament period, and preferably contemporary with the prophet, to whom such words as these could apply.[10]

The second great objection to this interpretation is that it does not and cannot do justice to the New Testament interpretation of the Suffering Servant. The consistent advocate of the view that Isa. 53 refers to and describes the experience of an actual person who lived in the Old Testament period, whether Moses or Zerubbabel or Eleazar or the prophet himself, or simply represents an ideal figure present in the mind of the prophet, cannot speak of an actual fulfilment in Jesus Christ. The word "fulfilment," unless it is practically emptied of all its real, historical significance, certainly includes the idea of *reference*. A prophecy cannot have its fulfilment in something or some person to which or to whom it has not the slightest reference. If the Servant was just as much an historical contemporary of the prophet as was Cyrus, if the prophet's words regarding the Servant referred to and had their fulfilment in this unknown contemporary just as his words regarding Cyrus had their fulfilment in Cyrus, then we have no more right to assert that the picture of the Suffering Servant in chap. 53 was prophetic of and was fulfilled in the sufferings of Christ, than that the triumphs of Cyrus were prophetic of and had their fulfilment in the triumph of Christ. We can speak of Jesus as a "second Jehoiachin" (supposing that for the sake of argument we accept the identification of the Servant with that ill-fated monarch) just as we could speak of Judas Maccabeus as a "second Cyrus," or of Eisenhower as a "second Foch," meaning simply that there are sufficient parallels, resemblances, correspondences, or analogies between the persons

---

[10] James D. Smart, in opposing the "collective" (Israel) interpretation of Isa. 53, has pointed out very clearly that to regard the sufferings of Israel as *vicarious* is quite inconsistent with the teachings of the prophets both as to the reason for these sufferings and as to the nature of Israel's mission to the nations. This leads him to insist that chap. 53 is to be sundered from 52:13-15 and that it and 50:4-10 are to be distinguished from the other "Songs" and regarded as referring to an individual. "In Chap. 53 the person who speaks in Chap. 50 is spoken about. He is described not by a mere onlooker, but by one who stands in a most intimate relationship to him." Consequently, Smart interprets both passages as referring directly to the prophet himself, whose martyr death tested the faith of his immediate followers to the utmost, and even led them to believe that by resurrection their master would share with them in the glories of the Day of Jehovah which they believed to be imminent. ("A New Approach to the Ebed-Yahweh Problem," *Expository Times* xlv, pp. 171f.).

whose names are thus linked together to justify the comparison.
But that would be all.[11]

The most that the consistent critic can do, if he wishes to
bridge the gap, which by his theory of prophecy he has created
between the Old Testament and the New, is to say that the New
Testament or the Christian Church has applied to persons and
events in the New Testament utterances which referred to and
had their realization in persons and events of the Old Testament
period. Thus he may say regarding Isaiah 53, "He may be the
whole nation, again the pious remnant of the nation, and at times
even an individual (a prophet)." He may even add "The Christian Church has seen the fulfilment of this chapter in Jesus
Christ, who, as God's perfect Servant, fulfilled in his sufferings
and death the experiences here described."[12] But he can do this
only if he shifts the responsibility for this interpretation wholly
on the "Christian Church." And if he is quite candid and honest
with himself and with those to whom he is presenting his view,
he will point out frankly that the reason the Christian Church
accepted the view that Isa. 53 has had its fulfilment in Jesus
Christ was because the Christian Church found this clearly
taught in the New Testament, and also because the Christian
Church has held throughout the centuries, and still holds, in so
far as her great creedal statements have not been made a dead
letter through the acceptance of the radical conclusions of negative criticism, a theory of prophecy which made it quite possible

[11] Thus Smart can tell us only that "The New Testament parallel is obvious"
between the sufferings of the Servant and the mission of Jesus Christ. What, on
his principles of interpretation, he cannot say is, that the prophecy foretold the
sufferings of Christ and had its fulfilment in Him; *parallel* and *fulfilment* are
quite different words. It is a law of mathematics that parallel lines never meet.
It is also to be noted that from the standpoint of evangelical truth, the "parallel"
drawn by Smart is a disastrous one. He tells us, "The writer of 53 regards
forgiveness, peace, and healing for himself and those for whom he speaks as
having been secured by the sufferings of the martyr." This means that the
Sufferer proclaimed these truths and suffered martyrdom as a result. "The
spiritual faith, however, of which his message had been the inspiration lived on
among his followers. It was found as the way of salvation by some who had
formerly remained aloof. Would it be astonishing for these men to say, 'He
suffered for us'? They owed all their spiritual life and hope to him, and his
sufferings and death had been the price of his remaining true to his message.
He did suffer for their sakes, that God's truth might be maintained for them
and so they might have peace and healing." Then the writer draws the N. T.
parallel: "The New Testament parallel is obvious. Jesus during His lifetime
proclaimed forgiveness, peace, and healing as already open to everyone who
would believe. His followers, however, regarded his sufferings and death as
having secured these for them" (*op. cit.*, p. 171). This can only mean that Jesus
proclaimed a salvation which was independent of His death, and that His disciples mistakenly made it dependent on His death; the Cross was a martyrdom
not an atonement for sin!

[12] *Westminster Study Edition*, p. 1015.

for her to speak of the New Testament *fulfilment* of Old Testament *prophecy*. But the consistent critic is on much safer ground and he is much less likely to be misunderstood, if he simply tells his reader, that Isa. 53 has been "applied" to the death of Christ, as in the case of Isa. 7:14 he has declared that that prophecy, "originally spoken of a birth in Isaiah's day," is in Matt. 1:23f. "applied to Jesus' birth."[13] "Applied" is sufficiently different from "fulfilled" to make clear to the discerning reader the vast difference between the Biblical and the Critical positions; and it avoids that ambiguous use of words which beclouds the issue and leads to confusion and misunderstanding.

A critic who holds that by the Servant the prophet meant the Israel of his own time may tell us that "his finest and deepest thoughts were understood by but few, until He came who embodied the ideal of the Servant of Yahweh in Himself: Jesus of Nazareth."[14] Or he may tell us that "Jesus Himself radically altered the Messianic idea by adding His cross to it, in the light of Isa. 53."[15] He may even speak of "instances of fulfilled presentiments" and of "close correspondences of events with prophetic anticipations."[16] But he will hesitate or refuse to speak definitely of *pre*diction and fulfilment of predicted events. The historian who treats Isa. 40-55 as contemporary history may conclude his meticulous study of it as such by saying of these chapters:

> "This attempt to find in these passages direct references to contemporary events in no way excludes the deeper meanings that attach to them. It merely serves to show that the prophet of cc. xl-lv was a man of the same stature as the Isaiah who prophesied in the time of Hezekiah, a religious leader facing the urgent political problems of his time with greater faith and courage, from a broader, less national, point of view than the majority in Israel could understand."[17]

What the "deeper meanings" of these prophecies may be, which this historian treats as contemporary documents dealing with current events, he does not tell us. But it is hard to avoid the conclusion that the more completely and perfectly these prophecies can be regarded as referring to and as fulfilled in contemporary events, the harder will it be to find a fulfilment in future events which is anything more than an analogy or parallel, history repeating itself. It is obvious that such a treatment

---

[13] See pp. 12 f. *supra*.

[14] J. A. Bewer, *The Literature of the Old Testament*, pp. 208f.

[15] T. H. Robinson, in *A Companion to the Bible* (1939, T. W. Manson, editor), pp. 327, 330.

[16] Cf. W. A. L. Elmslie, Article "Prophet" in *Encyclop. Brit.* (1929), p. 589.

[17] Sidney Smith, *op. cit.*, p. 75.

of these prophecies fits perfectly the definition of prophet referred to at the beginning of this study, as expressing the *critical* conception of the prophet and his work. He becomes indeed "a man of his own times," who "speaks to the people of his own times" regarding matters of "importance" to them. He becomes a sagacious statesman, who can read better the signs of the times than most of his contemporaries. But his concern is with the present and the immediate future. What use future generations may make of his words or how they may "apply" them to the altered and yet similar circumstances in which they will live, is a question with which he has no real concern. For, according to the consistent critic, "The Messianic interpretation is altogether contrary to the character of prophecy, which excludes prediction."[18]

THE INCONSISTENT CRITICAL POSITION

The serious consequences of the consistent application of the critical theory as to the nature of prophecy to Messianic prophecy in general and especially to the prophecies concerning the Servant, among which Isaiah 53 is preeminent, ought to be obvious to anyone who has any knowledge of or regard for the historic faith of the Christian Church or the New Testament interpretation of Old Testament prophecy, which the Church has always regarded as authoritative. Hence it was only to be expected that the attempt would be made—and it has been made again and again—by those who were willing or felt obliged to accept the general theory of the critics but were unwilling to follow it out to its logical conclusions, to bridge the gap between the traditional and the consistent critical positions, which simply means, to bridge the gap between Old Testament *prediction* and New

---

[18] North (*op. cit.*, p. 30) quotes these words from Hitzig's discussion of Isa. 53 (*Der Prophet Jesaja*, 1833, p. 577); and he speaks of them as "a remark which shows how deeply the newer criticism had been influenced by the rationalistic spirit of the *Aufklaerung*." They are more than a "remark." They are intended as a conclusive and unanswerable argument or statement of fact. Hitzig has mentioned and rejected the historical "individual" theory, the identification with "the prophets as a class," and the "pious minority" view of Paulus, in favor of the identification with "the nation as a whole." He rejects the Messianic interpretation with the words, "to the Messianic interpretation alone (*der messianischen Erklaerung allein*) . . . there is before everything else the objection (*steht vor allen Dingen entgegen*) that the nature (*Character*) of Prophecy excludes prediction." The word "alone" carefully restricts this objection to the *Messianic* interpretation. The words "before everything else" and "excludes" show how utterly Hitzig was opposed to the recognition of the prediction of any events which did not directly affect the prophet and his immediate audience (cf. *ibid.*, pp. 466f.). Basically there is little or no difference between Hitzig's principles of interpretation and the position taken many years later by Davidson, except that Hitzig was consistent in applying them and Davidson was not.

Testament *fulfilment*. For probably only the more extreme critics would be prepared to take definite exception to the words of Davidson: "There must be a connection between prophecy and fulfilment."[19]

The attempt to establish or retain such a connection on the basis of critical principles was made, for example, many years ago by George Adam Smith. His attempt is especially noteworthy because his *Commentary on Isaiah* (1888-90) probably did more to gain a hearing for, and to secure wide acceptance of, the theory of the multiple authorship of Isaiah among English-speaking readers than any other single book. Let us then briefly consider his interpretation of Isa.. 53, in the light of that critical theory regarding the *situation* and *scope* of prophecy of which he was so persuasive an advocate.

With regard to the *situation* of the Sufferer, Smith tells us: "In some verses he and his work seem already to have happened upon earth, but again we are made to feel that he is still future to the prophet, and that the voices, which the prophet quotes as speaking of having seen him and found him to be the Saviour, are voices of a day not yet born, while the prophet writes."[20] This is a singular and noteworthy statement, in view of its significant admissions. Note especially the words: "in some verses he and his work seem already to have happened upon earth." This means that to some extent at least, the situation is Calvary or later. Furthermore, the prophet "quotes" the testimony of "those who have seen him and found him to be the Saviour," which seems to mean that the prophet has not himself witnessed the sufferings of Christ, but "quotes" the testimony of those who have. How can he quote the testimony of those who witnessed a far-future event? Does not this amount to saying that he places himself among those witnesses? Clearly then the prophecy must deal, at least to a considerable extent, with a "non-existent situation." Whether the prophet is himself transported in vision to Calvary or receives through "voices" the testimony of eye-witnesses to the sufferings of Christ, the result is practically the same: the prophet describes the sufferings as having actually taken place. It is difficult to avoid the impression that had this writer been applying the words of this chapter to Cyrus instead of to the Messiah he would not have resorted to what looks very much like a mere verbal quibble, in order to avoid saying that the sufferings of the Servant are described as if by an eye-witness. We cannot but feel that Kennett, a consistent critic who dates

---

[19] *O. T. Prophecy*, p. 377.
[20] G. A. Smith, *op. cit.*, ii., pp. 366f.

Isa. 53 in the 2nd century B.C. and finds in it a description of the sufferings and triumphs of the Hasidim, has much the better of the argument when he says: "On this point it seems to me there is absolutely no room for doubt. A consideration of the tenses of the Hebrew verbs in this passage shows conclusively that the author is here stating *that the Servant of the Lord has already been smitten to death.* He is describing an historical fact."[21] For this forthright way of speaking is the way in which, as we have seen, Smith refers to the prophecies regarding Cyrus. The description of the sufferings of the Servant (53:1-10*a*) is entirely in terms of the past, though as we have seen it is set in a framework which tells of the glorious future to follow them. And we are convinced that Smith would have spoken in the same way of the sufferings of the Servant as he does of the victories of Cyrus, as present realities to the mind of the prophet, but for the fact that his acceptance of the critical theory as to the situation and scope of prophecy made it impossible for him to do this and at the same time to regard the prophecy as Messianic. For if the situation of the prophet is exilic and if he speaks of Calvary and of the sufferings of Calvary as already past, the theory of the critics that prophecy cannot deal with a "distant" and a "non-existent situation" and that the prophet cannot speak of future events as if they had already transpired, simply cannot be maintained.

The result is the same when we consider the attitude of this critic toward the *scope* of Old Testament prophecy. In arguing for the exilic date of chaps. 40-66, and with a view to reassuring the reader by proving that no doctrinal issue is involved, Smith declares that "ch. 53, as a prophecy of Jesus Christ, is surely as great a marvel if you date it from the Exile as if you date it from the age of Isaiah."[22] The answer to this claim would seem to be almost too obvious to mention. Isaiah 53, regarded as *a prophecy of Jesus Christ* is indeed *a great marvel,* if uttered in the 6th century B.C. It is a far greater marvel than is the Cyrus prophecy, regarded as a prediction of Cyrus uttered by Isaiah in the 8th or early 7th century B.C., some 150 years before Cyrus captured Babylon. This is quite true, obviously true. But the all-important thing to notice is that both of these interpretations involve *marvels* which the consistent critical student of prophecy cannot possibly accept. For if predictive prophecy can span the five centuries and more between "Deutero-Isaiah"

---

[21] R. H. Kennett, *The Servant of the Lord,* p. 93. Cf. the even more emphatic statement in his Schweich Lectures, *The Composition of the Book of Isaiah,* p. 72.

[22] *Op. cit.,* ii., p. 7.

and Calvary, it could certainly span the much shorter interval between Isaiah and the close of the Exile. If Isaiah 53 is really a Messianic prophecy, then it is undeniable that Old Testament prophecy can and does concern itself with events lying in the far-distant future. And this amounts to the admission that the prophets did not speak merely "to the people of their own time" about "things of importance" to them, but that they also could and at times actually did speak of things which were "a great while to come." We repeat, if "Deutero-Isaiah" could and did predict Calvary, then Isaiah could have predicted both Cyrus and Calvary. The scope of prophecy has been extended by this critic to include both.

Furthermore, if it is correct to say that Isaiah 53 applies to Jesus Christ in such a way and to such a degree that "in every essential of consciousness and of experience He was the counterpart, embodiment, and fulfilment of this Suffering Servant and His service,"[23] then in this prophecy we are not dealing with a vague and general prediction, which had only a vague and general fulfilment, or with an "ideal," or "anticipation," or "presentiment," which found an "analogy," a "correspondence," a "parallel" in some future event, but with the definite fulfilment of a definite prediction. Except for the mention of Cyrus by name, the correspondence between the Cyrus prophecies and the Servant prophecies as regards definiteness of portrayal is very great. So again we must conclude that if Deutero-Isaiah could have uttered the one, Isaiah could have uttered both. And the reverse of this proposition is equally true. If Isaiah could not have predicted Cyrus, neither Isaiah nor Deutero-Isaiah could have predicted the Messiah. In saying this we are simply saying what all really consistent critics will admit to be true.

What we are concerned to point out is, that in order to save the truly Messianic character of Isa. 53 and find for it a real fulfilment in the sufferings of Christ, this distinguished critic was obliged to surrender, or at least to modify so greatly as practically to invalidate, the two fundamental principles for the interpretation of prophecy which he and many others used so successfully to discredit the Isaianic authorship of the Cyrus prophecy and thereby to destroy the unity of Isaiah. The thoroughly consistent advocate of the critical conception of prophecy cannot believe that a prophet of the Exilic period could have spoken of Calvary in language so vivid that it suggests the eye-witness or the historian. He cannot believe that Isaiah 53

---
[23] *Ibid.,* p. 367.

was really a *prediction* of the sufferings of Christ, and that it really had its *fulfilment* in them. He cannot do this without surrendering the two great underlying principles which dominate his whole conception of the nature of prophecy.[24]

It is very important that the force of this argument should be fully appreciated. For it is only when it is fully grasped that the seriousness of the issue between the two conceptions of prophecy, the Biblical and the Critical, becomes fully apparent. Many Christians have been led astray at this very point. They have accepted the positive assertions of the inconsistent and mediating critics to the effect that no essential doctrine is involved in the question of the unity of Isaiah. They have imagined that they could continue to hold a truly Biblical conception of prophecy, that they could continue to believe that Isaiah 53 is truly Messianic and that it foretells the sufferings of Christ and was fulfilled in them, while accepting a theory which leads not only to the bisecting but to the dismemberment and disintegration of the book that passes under the name of Isaiah. But the whole trend of critical interpretation of prophecy as applied not only to Isaiah but to the entire prophetical portion of the Old Testament has been making it increasingly plain that there is no safe, that there is really no tenable, middle ground between the two positions. For the very arguments which deprive Isaiah of the authorship of the Cyrus prophecies must, if logically carried out, destroy the Messianic character of Isaiah 53, as well as of Old Testament prophecy as a whole.

A recent writer has stated the conclusion of the consistent critics in the following words: "There is nothing in the Old Testament which can properly be interpreted as a prediction of the Messiah of the New Testament."[25] This may sound startling and even preposterous to the student of the Bible who is not familiar with the confident conclusions of the thoroughgoing

---

[24] Other advocates of the critical theory regarding Isaiah have been quite as emphatic as was Smith in interpreting this chapter as Messianic. Thus, A. F. Kirkpatrick denounced Duhm's preterist interpretation, declaring that, "There is no prophecy in the whole Old Testament which offers a more convincing proof, not only of God's foreknowledge and purpose, but of His communication of it to men through His prophets" (*The Doctrine of the Prophets*, p. 394). What we are concerned to point out is that as an advocate of the Deutero-Isaiah theory Kirkpatrick was inconsistent, while Duhm was consistent.

[25] E. W. Heaton, *His Servants the Prophets*, p. 112. Hengstenberg pointed out more than a century ago (*Christology*, vol. i., p. 493) that in Eichhorn's *Allgem. Bibliothek der. bib. Lit.* it is admitted that the Messianic interpretation of Isa. 53 would soon be generally accepted by Biblical critics were it not that they were convinced that "the prophets predict nothing of the future, except what they could know and anticipate without any special divine revelation" (vol. vi., p. 655).

advocates of the critical position. But this writer is simply echoing the opinions of leading critics of a century ago and expressing with equal frankness the conclusions reached by the consistent critics of the present time. Certainly a theory which leads to such alarmingly destructive conclusions as the one just stated should be examined and tested with the utmost care. For it is the logical result of the application of a theory which exposes its true character. And the wise man will not start on a toboggan without first carefully considering where it is likely to land him.

CHAPTER VIII

THE BASIC ISSUE

It should be quite clear from the above discussion that the supremely important issue that has been raised by what we have every right to call the "modern" interpretation of prophecy, both in its general principles and also in its special application to the question of the unity of Isaiah, is as to whether *there is any close and vital connection between the Old Testament and the New, whether the great historic events of which we read in the Gospels can really be said to be the fulfilment of predictions recorded in the Old Testament.* A. B. Davidson declared many years ago as we have seen that, "There must be a connection between prophecy and fulfilment." To any one who accepts the statements of the New Testament at their face value, such a statement is so obvious as to be axiomatic. The Christian Church has accepted and defended this position, as clearly implied, for example, in the words, "that it might be fulfilled, which was spoken by the prophet." But we have seen that the unmistakable trend in critical circles has been to weaken or destroy that connection, to do this by adopting a definition of prophecy which makes prediction *ex hypothesi* practically impossible.

This fact is illustrated by the following statement regarding Isa. 53 which was made some years ago, but would apply equally well to the present situation: "The majority of Christian scholars now hold the Jewish interpretation that, though the picture is highly individualized, it still refers to the suffering nation."[1] This statement is too sweeping, even if the word "critical" were substituted for "Christian," as in all fairness should be done. For while, as we have seen, the "suffering nation" interpretation is widely held by critical scholars, there are other solutions which are or have been more or less popular. The reason for the quotation is that the writer did not hesitate to describe what he regarded as the most generally accepted *critical* interpretation as "the Jewish interpretation." It is important to note, therefore, that there is good and reliable evidence to show that this was not the original Jewish interpretation. The Targum of Jonathan, recognized as official by the Babylonian Talmud, begins 52:13 with the words, "Behold my servant, the Messiah, shall prosper." And there is other evidence that the Messianic interpretation

---

[1] W. G. Jordan, *Songs of Service and Sacrifice,* p. 137.

was current among the Jews in early times, despite the fact that the description of the humiliation, death, and resurrection of the Servant constituted a problem which they were naturally quite unable to solve. It was apparently not until the Middle Ages that distinguished Jewish scholars such as Rashi, Ibn Ezra, and the Kimchis adopted the "Israel" interpretation, although that interpretation was known as early as the time of Origen (3d cty.).[2] Insofar as they had the Christian interpretation in view,[3] their object in adopting this rival interpretation was to destroy the connection between the Old Testament prophecy and what they believed to be the mistakenly alleged fulfilment of it recorded in the New Testament, the death of Jesus of Nazareth.

A special reason for calling attention to this matter is that it raises the vitally important question, How can scholars who profess to be Christians accept an interpretation which is designed and intended to destroy the connection between the Old Testament, which they and the Jews accept, and the New Testament, which they accept and the Jews reject, and at the same time expect to maintain that connection between the two, which for centuries Christians, on the basis of the express claims of the New Testament, have regarded as perfectly obvious? How can they break down the bridge and maintain the connection intact? Or, are they ready to confess that the Jews are right in maintaining that there is no such connection, which must mean, of course, that the New Testament writers were mistaken when they so interpreted the prophecy? For the Jews, if they reject the Messianic interpretation, the question is simply, Who is referred to in the prophecy of the Suffering Servant? For the Christian, if he has any regard for the traditional belief of the Church or for the teaching of the New Testament, the question is a double one: if the prophecy is not a prediction of the sufferings of Christ, what is its import, *and how is its New Testament interpretation to be accounted for?*

One of the most recent discussions of this much debated question has been already referred to. It is by Prof. Christopher R. North of the University College of North Wales: *The Suffering Servant in Deutero-Isaiah: An Historical and Critical Study* (1948). In it the learned author sets forth the results

[2] Cf. Driver-Neubauer, *The Fifty-Third Chapter of Isaiah according to the Jewish Interpreters* (1876-7), with an Introduction by E. B. Pusey; also, G. H. Dalman, *Jesaia liii, Das Prophetenwort von Suhnleiden des Heilmittlers.* For a recent discussion see North, *op. cit.,* pp. 6-22.

[3] It was not of course the only reason. The "Israel" interpretation is very flattering to the national pride and the self-righteous spirit which is characteristic of many peoples and particularly of "the chosen people."

of a very careful examination and appraisal of the many and various theories which have been advanced for the solution of the problems which center about Isaiah 53.[4] In concluding his chapter on "Jewish Interpretations," he makes the following significant statement:

> "It is evident that the Jews themselves have been almost as perplexed about the Servant as Christians have been ever since, a century and a half ago, they abandoned the Messianic interpretation."

This statement should be read in connection with the opening sentences of the chapter entitled, "Christian Interpretations: From Doederlein to Duhm":

> "As long as it was believed that the Book of Isaiah was entirely the work of an eighth-century prophet, it was natural to assume that those portions of it which have an exilic background must be prophecy in the predictive sense of the word. Accordingly, the Messianic interpretation of the Servant seemed obvious. But no sooner was there talk of a Babylonian Isaiah than Christian scholars began to adopt the view that had long prevailed among the Jews, namely, that the Servant was the nation Israel. This collective theory has taken many forms."

Putting these two statements together, we note two matters which are of great significance and which are fully borne out by the evidence. The first is that, when the Messianic interpretation of this passage is rejected, its interpretation becomes a perplexing one. The second is, that, while the reasons for its rejection by Jewish and by Christian scholars were different, the result has been much the same for both. The Jews rejected the Messianic interpretation centuries ago, partly if not mainly, because it seemed to point to a fulfilment in Christ. But it was not until nearly the beginning of the last century that Christians began to question and reject this interpretation. Their reason for doing so was, as we have seen, the acceptance of a theory regarding prophecy—as being largely non-predictive—which logically made the Messianic interpretation impossible.

All of the substitutes which have been offered for the traditional Messianic interpretation are subjected to a careful and searching examination by Professor North. He definitely rejects all forms of the Historical Individual, the Mythological (Babylonian), and the Autobiographical interpretations; and he concludes that the correct solution is to be found in some form of the

[4] North tells us in his preface that there are at present only four interpretations which "still hold the fort." They are (1) the historical individual theory, "that the Servant was an anonymous contemporary of the Second Isaiah, a man who, the Prophet believed, was destined to be the Messiah"; (2) the autobiographical theory; (3) the collective theory which he finds to be most widely held in England; and (4) the Messianic theory (pp. 3f.).

Collective (Israel) theory. He inclines to the view that it is the ideal rather than the empirical Israel which the Prophet has in view; and, largely influenced by Peake and Wheeler Robinson, he decides in favor of the "corporate personality" form of this theory. This personalizing of a collective ideal he justifies on the ground that the Hebrews were disposed to think in terms of the concrete and personal, and not of the abstract or ideal. But this leads to the question, "Is, then, the interpretation still collective, or are we not back at what is essentially the traditional Messianic interpretation?" And this necessitates, of course, a final appraisal of the "traditional Messianic interpretation."[5] For, if the form of the *Israel* interpretation which he adopts resembles the *Messianic* interpretation as closely as Professor North's words would seem to indicate, the question naturally arises, Why cannot the critical interpreter of prophecy accept the traditional Messianic interpretation?

Professor North states his reasons for rejecting the traditional Messianic interpretation as follows:

"The fundamental objection to the traditional Messianic interpretation is that it is wedded to a too mechanical doctrine of inspiration. This seems to put it out of court as unworthy of serious consideration. The Prophet is a mere amanuensis, and what he writes has no relevance to the circumstances of his own time. Moreover, if this implies that he 'sees' in advance One who was not to come for another five or six centuries, it raises the difficult philosophical problem whether there can be an actual prevision of history."[6]

Since these objections are clearly regarded as cogent and conclusive for all those who with Professor North hold the critical theory regarding prophecy, they are deserving of very careful consideration:

---

[5] *Ibid.*, p. 207.

[6] *Ibid.*, p. 207f. It is to be noted that North believes that what he regards as the "fundamentalist" or literalist form of the Messianic interpretation has been abandoned by an increasing number of its advocates, and that "the traditional form of the Messianic interpretation has given place to one more realistic, which fully recognizes that the conception of the Messiah-Servant arose out of the personal and historical circumstances in which the Prophet found himself, and that, therefore, there need not be entire congruence between the prophecy and its fulfilment in Christ." He feels that "There are, of course, correspondences, but there are also differences," and that "The problem of exact photographic prevision of the future does not, therefore, arise. The essential likeness between the Servant and Jesus lies in this: that whereas prophets like Jeremiah suffered in the course of, or as a result of, their witness, for both the Servant and Jesus suffering is the means whereby they fulfil their mission and bring it to a triumphant conclusion." "This conception," he tells us, "is unique in the Old Testament." As to this it seems sufficient to remark that if this "essential likeness" adequately expressed the Messianic interpretation, it is hard to see why Professor North should find any difficulty in accepting it.

(1) The first objection is that the traditional view is "wedded to a too mechanical doctrine of inspiration," which is explained to mean that the prophet is "a mere amanuensis." As to this objection we observe that, if Professor North had examined the doctrine of inspiration held by those who believe in the Messianic interpretation of Isa. 53 with the same meticulous care which he has given to the consideration of the various critical theories, he would not have given a definition of it which is emphatically repudiated by its ablest advocates, namely, the "dictation" theory of inspiration.

In saying this we are not taking the position that for a finite, mortal man to act as *amanuensis* for Almighty God would be quite so unworthy an office as Professor North seems to think. If a communication is weighty and momentous, especially if it is of heavenly origin, the most important thing, we may even say, the all-important thing in connection with it would be *accuracy of transmission*. Many a merely human message has been weakened, garbled, falsified, or made unintelligible by the stupidity, ignorance, forgetfulness, or self-importance of the messenger. "Learning by rote" is much decried today; and it is quite true that a rule which is simply learned but not mastered may be almost useless. But when a pupil puts "in his own words" the carefully stated rule given in his lesson-book, it is often conspicuously lacking in the precision and clarity of the original and may miss the point or obscure the meaning. When the adjutant brings an officer a message from the commander-in-chief, what that officer needs most of all to know, especially if the situation is critical, is this, "Is this exactly what the supreme commander said?" And if it is a written order, signed by the commander himself, so much the better. Whether it is derogatory to the adjutant to act as messenger boy is of relatively minor importance. The message itself is the all-important thing. Hamlet's words to the players, "Speak the speech, I pray you, as I pronounced it to you" are often quoted. But an older statement of the duty of the spokesman or messenger is this: "he that hath my word, let him speak my word faithfully" (Jer. 23:28). The critics may regard what they call the "dictation" theory as "unworthy of serious consideration." But there is not one of them, who would not wish and endeavor, if he needed to send an important message, to entrust it to a messenger who could be depended on to deliver it correctly, even if this involved repeating it "word for word" as he received it or even the putting of it in writing; and he would probably consider the question whether it was beneath the dignity of his messenger to carry a verbal or a written message, a matter of little consequence. The message is the main thing, not the messenger.

It is also to be remembered, that a theory of inspiration which is neither plenary nor verbal cannot do justice to the authority of the prophet and the certitude of his message. Unless we can be sure that the *words* in which the message is contained correctly state and express that message, all attempts to determine what the message really is may be useless and worse than useless. The painstaking effort which Biblical scholars expend on the task of determining the exact meaning of the sentences, phrases, and single words of the Biblical text would be largely wasted if the sentences and phrases and single words cannot be trusted to convey the meaning of the Sender. A general inspiration, which did not guarantee the accuracy of sentences, phrases, and words would make thoroughly scientific study of the Bible, as a message from God, practically impossible.

But, it is to be carefully noted and should be recognized by the opponents of this view that those who hold the doctrine of plenary verbal inspiration, at least its best and ablest advocates, insist that their doctrine is not a mere dictation theory. On the contrary, they maintain that God in speaking through the prophets used them not as automatons and robots but as men; that in doing so He respected and made use of their differences in personality, temperament, circumstance and situation, station, training, culture, experience; indeed, that He formed and fashioned them by heredity, environment, and special training to be just the kind of messengers that He needed for the purposes which He had in view. In the case of Jeremiah we are expressly told that this Divine preparation and training entered into his very being, that God's purpose to use Jeremiah was formed prior to Jeremiah's conception in the womb (Jer. 1:4-7). He felt himself a child, but God made him His spokesman to a nation. Jeremiah was fully conscious that the message which he declared had come to him from God; and he denounced as false prophets those who spoke a message out of "their own hearts." How it can be that the same word is both the word of God and the word of an Isaiah, of a Jeremiah, of an Ezekiel, we cannot fully understand. But it is clear that the Bible so represents it; and to deny either of these plainly stated factors is to come dangerously short of doing full justice to the nature of prophecy and

the function of the prophet as they are set forth in the Bible.[7]
(2) The second reason for rejecting as too mechanical that
theory regarding prophecy which interprets this chapter as directly Messianic is that such a prophecy if uttered by Deutero-
Isaiah five or six centuries before the Crucifixion would have "no
relevance to the circumstances of his own time."[8] This is, as
we have seen, the argument from *situation*. A single example
will suffice to show its inadequacy as applied to Isa. 40-66 of
which chap. 53 forms so important a part. North tells us that
"The Songs are quite evidently born of an intense anguish of soul,
anguish such as the Prophet must have experienced when Cyrus,
whom he expected to be a kind of first-fruits of Yahweh among
the Gentiles, proclaimed instead his enthusiasm for Bel-Marduk."[9] We have already pointed out that there is no sufficient
warrant for this theory of the prophet's disappointment in Cyrus.
It fails to take account of the words, "though thou hast not
known me," used by the prophet in speaking of the Persian and
his mission; and it derives its cogency entirely from the assumption that the prophet was an actual contemporary of Cyrus.

---

[7] One of the ablest defenders of this doctrine of Scripture was the late Professor B. B. Warfield of Princeton. He stated it briefly as follows: "Every word
of the Bible is the word of God according to the doctrine we are discussing; but
also and just as truly, every word is the word of man." This is due to the fact
that God is "the God of providence and of grace as well as of revelation and
inspiration." Hence "If God wished to give His people a series of letters like
Paul's, He prepared a Paul to write them, and the Paul He brought to the task
was a Paul who spontaneously would write just such letters." Warfield states
the reason for the claim of the critics that "we cannot get from a man a pure
word of God" as follows: "As light that passes through the colored glass of
a cathedral window, we are told, is light from heaven, but is stained by the
tints of the glass through which it passes, so any word of God which is passed
through the mind and soul of a man must come out discolored by the personality
through which it is given and just to that degree ceases to be the pure word of
God." He answers it partly in terms of this striking rhetorical question: "But
what if this personality has itself been formed by God into precisely the personality it is, for the express purpose of communicating to the word given through
it just the coloring which it gives it?" (*The Inspiration and Authority of the
Bible*, pp. 437, 155f.). In short, just as the color scheme of the window is due to
the design of the artist and its variety and diversity the evidence of his skill and
artistry, so the various ways in which the human element appears in the divine
revelation show the great variety in the human agents which God used to convey
His messages to men. Such a view of inspiration may properly be called both
"verbal" and "plenary." It is not a "dictation" theory. Cf. Charles Hodge, *Sys-
tematic Theology*, i., pp. 156f., 164ff.

[8] This also shows how difficult North finds it to understand the Messianic interpretation. For obviously a message through an "amanuensis" could be quite
as *timely* and quite as *appropriate to the contemporary scene* as a message which
the prophet put in his own words or even one which he thought out himself.
This must be so, unless we are to infer that the prophet must have been better
informed regarding the existing situation than the God in whose name he pro-
fessed to speak!

[9] *Op. cit.*, p. 217.

What concerns us in this connection is the fact, referred to above, that the Book of Isaiah describes another situation for these prophecies which has very definite relevance to the circumstances of the prophet's own time.

We have already seen that, according to the arrangement of chapters in Isa. 36-39, the ominous prediction of bondage to Babylon stands immediately before the Book of Consolation. The natural inference is that the one served as the occasion for the other. Those who find the occasion of the "Songs" in Deutero-Isaiah's disappointment in Cyrus should certainly be willing to do full justice to the anguish of mind with which Isaiah himself must have pondered the tragic message which he brought to Hezekiah after the ambassadors of Merodach-baladan had left him. The terrible prediction was uttered soon after Hezekiah's first deliverance from Sennacherib. But we cannot tell whether the message of comfort which follows immediately in the Book of Isaiah was given to the prophet at once or perhaps months or even years later. Nor can we decide with certainty whether it all came to him at one time or at intervals during an extended period of time. But in either case, the close connection between the prophecy of doom and the message of comfort is indicated by the juxtaposition. It may also be noted that the confidence with which the prophet assured Hezekiah that Jerusalem should not fall into the hands of Sennacherib (37:22-35) becomes all the more remarkable when we remember that he had already long before this declared quite as emphatically to Hezekiah that his kingdom was to fall a victim to Babylon.[10]

On the basis of the traditional interpretation, the words of the Book of Consolation have their occasion in the ominous prophecy of slavery to Babylon, and they have relevance, indeed they have definite reference, to all the dark days which are to come upon God's people. And just as during the lifetime of Isaiah the dark shadow which is cast over the future by 39:6f. is temporarily relieved by the signal triumph over Sennacherib recorded in chaps. 36-37, so in the Book of Consolation we find both threatenings and promises, rebuke and comfort, a message which is not limited in its scope to the Babylonian Captivity, but the great burden of which is the Messianic Age, a group of prophecies in which the people of God, the Old Testament Church and the New Testament Church, have found warning and counsel and comfort both for days of trial and for those of triumph.

---

[10] See above, Chap. III, note 22.

(3) The third reason that is given for rejecting the "traditional Messianic" interpretation of Isa. 53 is the most significant of all: it raises the "difficult philosophical problem" whether there can be "an actual prevision of history." This is of course the very heart and core of the whole problem of predictive prophecy. If there can be no actual prevision of history, the traditional view of prophecy must be rejected and its application to Isa. 53 must be definitely set aside, cost what it may. It is of first importance, therefore, to note that Professor North speaks of it as "a difficult philosophical problem." For the solution of this problem he turns to Plato and what is known as the "Platonic" or "philosophic" myth.[11] He accepts the definition of such a myth which is given by C. C. J. Webb.[12] It is "a story," which is "quite likely to be untrue—nay, even quite unlikely to be true in detail," but which is "in the Platonic phrase 'like the truth,' because it is controlled by our knowledge, obtained through Philosophy, of that fundamental nature of the universal system which any event falling within it must of necessity exemplify." This, it will be observed, makes of the Old Testament prophet a philosopher who interprets the times in which he lives in terms of his knowledge of "the fundamental nature of the universal system." If he regards this system as fundamentally moral, he will interpret all events, past, present, and future, in terms of moral inevitability; and only in this sense will the words "prophet" and "predict" be suitable in dealing with the phenomena of the Bible.

Pfleiderer stated much the same view many years ago in his book, *The Philosophy of Religion* (1888). Applying it to Isa. 53, he has told us: "This was not intended as a Messianic prophecy of Christ—the prophet is not speaking of things future, but of things present—yet it was in fact such a prophecy, since it contained an eternal truth which fulfils itself again and again in history, but never did so more grandly, or with more far-reaching consequences, than in the Sufferer on Golgotha. Deutero-Isaiah has thus a good right to be called the evangelist of the Old Testament."[13] This amounts to saying that prophecy is to be understood as the declaration of "eternal truth" or of "the fundamental nature of the universal system" which may confidently be expected to find concrete expression or embodiment "again and again" in the events of history. But when or how these principles will find such concrete expression and to what

---

[11] *Ibid.*, p. 212.
[12] *God and Personality* (1918), p. 170.
[13] Vol. iii, p. 148.

extent they will express or exemplify such "eternal truth" must apparently remain quite uncertain. For, according to Webb, the "story" which the philosopher-prophet tells "is quite likely to be untrue—nay, even quite unlikely to be true in detail."

How such a theory, whether we call it "philosophical" or "mythical" might apply to Biblical prophecy, and how inadequate it would be to account for it, is illustrated by two quite parallel, yet also, in a sense, strikingly dissimilar examples. Isaiah and Jeremiah both believed in a God who was supremely moral and who would punish His people if they refused to obey His holy laws. Isaiah denounced the sins of Judah and Jerusalem as severely as Jeremiah did, if not more severely. When Sennacherib sent a detachment of his army to demand the surrender of Jerusalem, Isaiah met the demand with high defiance and declared that Jerusalem should be inviolable. And it was so! When Nebuchadnezzar was thundering at the gates of Jerusalem and such a ringing message as Isaiah had uttered seemed to the patriotic leaders to be imperative, Jeremiah, we are told, "weakened the hands" of his compatriots who were manfully resisting the enemy by declaring that the king of Babylon was the Lord's Servant, that the city should inevitably fall into his hands, and that the only hope of safety lay in surrendering to him and serving him. He even went so far as to delimit the period of servitude to seventy years. And it was so! It is true, in a sense, that both of these prophets prophesied in terms of that "fundamental nature of the universal system" which is made so plain in the Bible, to wit, that God is righteous yet merciful, severe yet loving, angry yet patient, that he both punishes and forgives. But if that was all, how did Isaiah know that his God would spare a sinful people and deliver them in their hour of need? How did Jeremiah know that his God, who was also Isaiah's God, would not spare but would destroy His city and the temple which had been made for Him to dwell in? Was it because Isaiah and Jeremiah differed radically in their understanding of the fundamental nature of the universal system? Or was it because their respective situations differed so radically that the "particular event" which the one foresaw as of *necessity* exemplifying the universal system was deliverance, while for the other it was captivity? And if what they both foretold was "quite likely to be untrue" and "quite unlikely to be true in detail," how are we to account for the amazing confidence with which both alike proclaimed their messages as the Word of the Lord, and for the further fact that both of them were proved to be true prophets by the outcome of events?[14] We would think that according to the theory we are discussing the chances of such accurate fulfilment would be slight indeed.[15] North seems to admit this when he says: "The Songs are myth—provisional or anticipated history—not allegory."[16] "Provisional" and "anticipated" acquire a decidedly sinister meaning in the light of the words quoted above.

In view of the seriousness of the issue with which we are dealing, it is very unfortunate that words of recognized and precious meaning are often used in a sense which is either so diluted or so different from what has in the past been regarded as their proper and only true significance, that a quite false impression is given of the position of the one who uses them. This is particularly true of the word "Messianic." Messianic in its proper sense means "relating to the Messiah." "Messiah" is the Hebrew word which appears in the New Testament as "Christ." According to the New Testament and that Christian faith which is built upon it, Messianic, in the broad and proper sense of the word, means *Christian*. It is the great word which binds the Old Testament and the New Testament together, as both alike testifying to Jesus the Christ, the Son of God, the Saviour of the world. But for those who do not believe in predictive prophecy and for whom the idea of "an actual prevision of history" is a philosophical problem which is difficult if not impossible of solution, the word Messianic tends to lose its real meaning and to stand for little if any more than that "golden age" expectancy, which refuses to accept as final and inevitable the tragic failures which have marked in the past and are marking today the course of human history, and insists on hitching

---

[14] Riehm (*Messianic Prophecy*, 1891, p. 19) makes a telling comment on Duhm's explanation of the amazing accuracy of Isaiah's prophecies. According to Duhm, as quoted by Riehm, "The simple means which produced this result—the source from which the prophet's political wisdom flowed—was nothing more than the *belief that Jehovah was directing the affairs of all nations into the channels of His purpose for His own people.*" Riehm points out that "the consideration, that many have held this belief without being able to give an infallible judgment on coming events might have convinced him that his own explanation of the 'great result' is wholly insufficient." But it is to be remembered that the thoroughgoing critic does not really believe in predictive prophecy of any kind. Riehm himself accepted the critical theory of two (or more) Isaiahs, but did not follow it out to its logical results.

[15] Abraham made use of the "moral inevitability" argument when he said, "Shall not the God of all the earth do right?" (Gen. 18:25). But this conviction did not enable him to envisage the actual situation in Sodom correctly; and the cities of the plain were destroyed in spite of his intercession.

[16] *Op. cit.*, p. 216.

its wagon to a star.[17] It may easily become simply another name for that development or progress toward the Superman which the evolutionist used to consider so inevitable as to be axiomatic, but which the course of recent events has proved to be so tragically illusory.

The same applies to the word "eschatological." It is frequently employed by men to whom the whole idea of predictive prophecy in the Biblical sense of that word is decidedly offensive. Eschatology is the science of the last things, the things which are to come. Yet many who have adopted a theory regarding prediction which makes foreknowledge of coming events practically impossible, continue to speak of Biblical or of Old Testament "eschatology." We have noted that Professor North finds a very serious difficulty with the "traditional Messianic interpretation" to be that it proceeds on the assumption that prevision of the future, even the distant future, is both possible and actual, a fact of history and experience, while he represents it as a "difficult philosophical problem." Yet we find that he draws a rather sharp distinction between Biblical eschatology and heathen myths. Speaking of the Hebrews he tells us:

> "Their emphasis was upon the concrete and historical, and purely mythological conceptions would have been abhorrent to them. They firmly believed in a divine purpose being wrought out in history, and consequently they developed an eschatology. The surrounding nations, on the other hand, had abundance of myth and drama, but no conception of God at work in history, and, consequently, no clearly attested eschatology."[18]

This statement which we believe to be historically and factually correct is significant because it at once raises the question, as to how the Hebrews came by this firm belief in "a divine purpose being wrought out in history." If their knowledge of the future was as dim, as vague, as illusory, as theoretical, as that of other nations and peoples—there may be very considerable difference between Babylonian mythology and Platonic myth, but essentially they are the same—how does it happen that the Hebrews alone developed a clearly attested eschatology? Is not the answer to be found in that very fact to which the Bible so constantly testifies, that they were given through their prophets a foresight and insight into the future, which was unique and was granted to no other people? The only adequate basis for Hebrew escha-

---

[17] Warfield described the situation a generation ago by saying: "Meanwhile, it is an unhappy fact that we may search in vain through many current treatises on the Messianic hope for intimations that it included the promise of a Divine Redeemer" ("The Divine Messiah in the Old Testament," *Princeton Theol. Review*, vol. xiv, p. 415).

[18] *Op. cit.*, p. 201.

tology is Hebrew prophecy. When their prophets, speaking in the name of the Lord, foretold things to come and those things came to pass, it was only natural for the devout in Israel to cherish a firm belief in a divine Providence controlling them and a divine purpose being wrought out in the course of their history. There is no other adequate explanation of this firm belief. And we have seen that the great argument in Isa. 40-48 for the sole and unique Deity of the God of Israel is that He is both able to foretell and to fulfil, and that by doing both He proves the idols of the heathen to be but things of naught.

Furthermore, it may be regarded as self-evident, we believe, that if there is a God who controls human affairs and is ordering the course of human events for the accomplishment of His purposes, it would be possible and even probable that He would give to men, especially to those individuals or that nation, which He purposed to use more particularly for the carrying out of those purposes, some prior knowledge of what those purposes were. Acceptance of the principle of a divine teleology or eschatology stands in very close and intimate relation to the question of predictive prophecy. Unless that divine purpose is so feeble as to be ineffectual, so vacillating as to be quite uncertain, so indefinite as to be meaningless, it should be both foreknowable and foretellable. Otherwise, to speak of eschatology in terms of divine purpose tends to become merely an empty phrase.

It is a significant fact that many scholars who accept in general the critical view regarding prophecy nevertheless find it difficult to avoid the recognition of the predictive element in it. Thus Pfleiderer, while denying that Deutero-Isaiah foresaw the sufferings of Christ, speaks of "the eagle eye of Jeremiah" seeing "on the distant horizon the dawn of a new covenant of religion made inward."[19] But he insists that "such flashes of light in which the mind flies over centuries are only granted to chosen spirits in the excitement of the most momentous times; when the storm of the time sinks to rest this rising of the spirit is followed by an ebb." All will admit that such "flashes of light" are rare. True prophecy is, speaking generally, a rare phenomenon. Biblical prophecy is a distinctive and unique feature of Biblical religion. But if such flashes of light are true and deal with reality, does not this mean that predictive prophecy, whether rare or frequent is not the question, is both possible and also an actual fact of experience?

North believes regarding Isa. 53 that the prophet "saw Reality in a few brief but vivid flashes, and he pictured what he saw,

[19] *Op. cit.*, vol. iii., p. 145.

not indeed in a portrait photographically correct, but full and exact enough for Jesus to recognize it as pointing to Himself."[20] To the question, "Can we discern a divine purpose in this?" his answer is, "I believe we can." And he concludes his entire discussion with these words: "I find it hard to believe that the Prophet in his moments of deepest insight intended one thing and the Holy Spirit another. It seems more natural to conclude that both intended the same. Original and Fulfilment join hands across the centuries." Why does Professor North regard this conclusion as "more natural"? He has indicated at least two reasons quite plainly. He cannot escape the conclusion that Isa. 53 has its only adequate realization in Calvary; and he cannot avoid the further conclusion that the course of Biblical history can only be understood as eschatological and Messianic. His words, "prophet . . . Holy Spirit," and "Original . . . Fulfilment," might seem to suggest that the prophet was solely concerned with the original and the Holy Spirit solely concerned with the fulfilment. But this is clearly not his meaning. What he intends to tell us is that the reason original and fulfilment join hands across the centuries is because the same Holy Spirit who brought about the fulfilment was also active in the disclosure of the original. Either this must be so, and if it is so, then we can speak of a real prediction and a real fulfilment, both brought about by the working of the one and self-same Spirit; or we must say with the poet, "There's a Divinity that shapes our ends, Rough hew them how we may" and limit the activities of that Divinity simply to the fulfilment of the words which the prophet uttered on his own initiative, as when we say, "Man proposes and God disposes"; or we must say that the connection between original and fulfilment is merely fortuitous, that they join hands across the centuries purely by accident and chance. Professor North finds it more natural to decide in favor of a "divine purpose."

It is especially important to observe that Professor North in offering his solution of the problem of Isa. 53 is doing so in terms of philosophic or Platonic myth, with full recognition of the fact that "actual prevision of the future is a difficult philosophical problem." He does not deal with it as a strictly Biblical problem. He does not appeal to a single one of the predictions we have discussed in Chap. I, a chain of more than a score of prophecies beginning in Genesis and running on to Daniel. It is to Platonic myth that he turns for support of a future refer-

[20] *Op. cit.*, p. 218.

ence of Isa. 53. He tells us, "Webb is cautious as to 'whether the future can ever be foreseen,' but that does not alter the fact that many myths do relate to the future: the *Phaedrus* Myth, for example, and the Divina Commedia of Dante; and if Plato had developed Glaucon's prophecy of the fate of the just man, we might have had a myth strikingly similar to Isa. liii."[21] He finds "another possible parallel" in the fourth Eclogue of Vergil; and he quotes apparently with approval R. S. Conway's comment, "Understood in the only way possible to the mind of the early centuries, that Eclogue made him a direct prophet, and therefore an interpreter of Christ."[22] And North's conclusion is: "If there was to be any anticipation of Calvary in the Old Testament—as, on any showing, there is in Isa. liii—it is difficult to see what form it could take except one analogous to Platonic myth." Professor North has all of the Old Testament and New Testament with their numerous records of prediction and fulfilment before him. Yet he turns to Plato and Vergil for proof that such a prophecy as Isa. 53 may really be a prediction dealing with the future, a prediction in the sense of myth, defined as "provisional or anticipated history."

This may seem remarkable, even amazing, to many readers. But the reason for it is not far to seek. It is also a most significant one. It is found in the simple fact that Professor North has adopted the "critical" theory of prophecy, a theory which proceeds upon the assumption that prediction, at any rate the prediction of the remote future, is improbable or impossible, and that therefore every evidence of its occurrence in the Bible must be regarded as suspicious and self-condemning, and must be eliminated or silenced, cost what it may. We have cited example after example to show the ways in which the critics have endeavored to eliminate prediction from prophecy. And we have also seen that this can be brought about only at the cost of discrediting and rejecting the express statements to the contrary made in the Bible itself. When this method of "interpretation" is carried out thoroughly, but only then, the critic can say: "There is nothing in the Old Testament which can properly be interpreted as a prediction of the Messiah of the

---

[21] *Op. cit.*, p. 212f.
[22] R. S. Conway, *Ancient Italy and Modern Religion* (last paragraph). His final words are, "and it is not the deepest students of Vergil who have thought him unworthy of such a ministry." When T. F. Royds tells us that "the most radical criticism brings us back to the old view that Vergil like Isaiah was a real prophet of Christ" (*Vergil and Isaiah*, pp. 46f.), what he is really telling us is that Isaiah was no more of a prophet than was Vergil, whose glorious picture of the future of the house of Augustus had its fulfilment in Nero, the last of the Caesars who could lay claim to descent from Trojan Iulus.

New Testament." And for those who accept this conclusion, predictive prophecy is largely if not wholly eliminated from the Bible and the critic must turn elsewhere—Professor North turns to Platonic myth—for proof of its existence.

The results of this method of dealing with Biblical prophecy have recently been stated by Professor Millar Burrows as follows:

"For many events, to be sure, we have abundant evidence of their occurrence in addition to the biblical record, but unless the statement that they had been predicted is accepted on the authority of the Bible itself, there is nothing to prove that the supposed prediction was not written after the event took place. In other cases, where the prophecy was demonstrably written before the event which is traditionally regarded as its fulfilment, the interpretation is open to question, if not obviously false. This is true of the prophecies supposed to be predictions of the birth, life, death, and resurrection of Jesus, and used as such in the New Testament itself, from Mt. 1:22f. on."[23] .

This is a very significant statement. For it reminds us of a most important fact: the only proof of the actual occurrence of predictive prophecy in the Bible is contained in the *Bible itself.* If then the evidence supplied by the Bible can be disposed of, there is no proof whatsoever of such occurrence. In the case of predictions which were (allegedly!) fulfilled in Old Testament times, all that is necessary is to deny that the alleged prediction was uttered before the event which fulfilled it. In the case of Old Testament prophecies which find their fulfilment in the New Testament, since it is impossible to deny that they were uttered before the event, it is to be held that the *Biblical interpretation* which treats the New Testament event as the fulfilment of an Old Testament prediction is to be regarded as "open to question, if not obviously false." And the advocate of this drastic treatment of the Bible concludes with the assertion that "The argument from prophecy will not convince any intelligent and informed person who does not already believe that the Bible is inspired."

It is to be noted, therefore, that it is not only the inspiration of the Biblical writers which is challenged by this treatment of the Bible, but also their trustworthiness and credibility as simple historians. For not only is the correctness of their interpretation of the prophecies called in question, but the very fact that they recorded them as predictions. This is clearly indicated by the claim that there is "nothing to prove that the supposed prediction was not written after the event took place." Nothing, except the fact that the Bible records them as such! The question is

---

[23] *Op. cit.,* p. 17f.

not, When were they written down? but rather, Is the statement
that they were predictions true or are they fabrications, history
written in the guise of prophecy after the alleged fulfilment?
And if the statements of simple fact of the Biblical writers are
rejected, their interpretations will naturally carry little weight.
They will be regarded as "open to question, if not absolutely
false." And in order that the reader may not have the slightest
doubt as to the implication and application of his words, this
author tells us: "This is true of the prophecies supposed to be
predictions of the birth, life, death, and resurrection of Jesus,
and used as such in the New Testament itself, from Mt. 1:22f.
on." The words, "from Mt. 1:22f. on," make it quite clear that
a "clean sweep" is to be made of every "interpretation" in the
New Testament which finds in the Old Testament a prediction of
the events which it records. This means, as we have already
seen, that the words of Matt. 1:22, "Now all this was done that
it might be fulfilled which was spoken of the Lord by the
prophet," which introduce the quotation of Isaiah. 7:14, are to
be understood to mean that the New Testament writer simply
"applied" to the birth of Jesus a somewhat similar event which
took place within nine months of the day when it was uttered.
It means that the story of the coming of the Magi (2:1-12) is
to be treated as a "parable" or as a "Christian Midrash rather
than authentic history."[24] And similar treatment must be
accorded to all the "supposed" predictions of "the birth, life,
death, and resurrection of Jesus" as they lie before us in the
"New Testament itself."

If predictive prophecy is to be eliminated from the Bible by
such methods as the ones referred to above, then it follows
inevitably, that for those who accept the conclusions of the critics
there is no valid *Biblical* evidence for such predictions and fulfilments as are recorded in the Bible, and *actual prevision of
the distant future* ceases to be a *Biblical fact* and becomes
instead a *difficult philosophical problem;* and, we must add, it
raises a question which is foredoomed to be answered in the
negative for the obvious reason that it is the denial of the possibility of such predictive prophecy which is directly responsible
for the drastic methods resorted to by the critics to eliminate
such prophecy from the Bible itself. Here we have the explanation, the only possible explanation of the fact that a critical
writer who clearly desires to find a connection between Isa. 53
and Calvary, who feels that Original and Fulfilment really do
"join hands across the centuries," finds himself obliged to go to

_____
[24] See above, pp. 12 f, 16.

Plato and Vergil instead of to the Bible to prove it. What could demonstrate the disastrous results of the critical treatment of Biblical prophecy more completely than this?

William Paley's *Evidences of Christianity* (1794) is probably seldom read today, although this little book was very popular several generations ago. Paley includes among the "auxiliary evidences of Christianity" to which he appeals a relatively brief chapter on "Prophecy." In it he limits himself to two examples, one from the Old Testament, the other from the New. They are the prophecy of the Suffering Servant (Isa. 52:13-53:12) and the prediction of the destruction of Jerusalem (Lk. 21:5-25). These he clearly regards as outstanding examples of Biblical prophecy. But it is to be noted that before introducing the argument from the fulfilment of prophecy, Paley has devoted nearly half of the first part of his treatise to the presentation of *eleven* arguments to prove that the Scriptures are *authentic*. This means that Paley saw quite as clearly as does the author quoted above that the claim of the Bible to record true examples of the "actual prevision of the distant future" must stand or fall on the reputation of the Bible as a trustworthy recorder and interpreter of the events with which it deals. In dealing with this question the primary consideration is the dependability of the Bible as a trustworthy record. And the most damaging indictment that can be brought against the Higher Criticism is that in endeavoring to eliminate predictive prophecy from the Bible it does not hesitate to assert or suggest that many of its predictions are simply pre-dated history, and that its interpretations of other of these predictions are "open to question, if not obviously false."

How contrary this attitude is to the spirit and the express teachings of the Bible, and how destructive it is in its tendencies, should be perfectly obvious to every intelligent reader of the Scriptures. In his presentation of the Christian doctrine of the resurrection of the body and the evidence for it (1 Cor. 15), the Apostle Paul begins as follows:

"Moreover, brethren, I declare unto you the gospel which I preached unto you, which also ye received, and wherein ye stand; by which also ye are saved, if ye keep in memory what I preached unto you, unless ye have believed in vain. For I delivered unto you first of all that which also I received, how that Christ died for our sins according to the scriptures; and that he was buried, and that he rose again the third day according to the scriptures; and that . . ."

It is significant that Paul begins his argument with an appeal to the Old Testament, to the fulfilment of prophecy. The mighty events of which he is about to speak have come about "according to the scriptures." His first appeal is to prophecy, to the testimony of those who being dead yet speak. It will hardly be questioned that for the atonement of Christ Paul had primarily in mind the 53rd of Isaiah, viewed in the light of the Mosaic ritual of sacrifice and the passover; and that like John the Baptist he saw in Jesus "the Lamb of God which taketh away the sin of the world." For the resurrection, he may have been thinking of the passages appealed to by Peter on the day of Pentecost as well as of others. But what is especially significant is that to establish the truth of these great doctrines of that Gospel which he preached to Jew and Gentile alike, the death and resurrection of the Lord Jesus Christ, Paul's first appeal is to the Scriptures of the Old Testament. Then he passes on to mention the living witnesses: Cephas, the twelve, the above five hundred brethren of whom "the greater part remain until this present," and so on. That is his order here. It was his order elsewhere. We may call it the New Testament order. The appeal to the Old Testament in support of the claims of the New is one of the most pervasive features of the New Testament Scriptures. And the reason for this emphasis is stated nowhere more plainly than in the words of the risen Lord as recorded in Luke 24. To the two disciples on the road to Emmaus Jesus said, "O fools and slow of heart to believe all that the prophets have spoken: Ought not Christ to have suffered these things, and to enter into his glory?" And the evangelist adds these words: "And beginning with Moses and all the prophets, he expounded unto them in all the scriptures the things concerning himself." And on the evening of this same resurrection day He said to the Ten as they were gathered together, "These are the words which I spake unto you, while I was yet with you, that all things must be fulfilled which were written in the law of Moses, and in the prophets, and in the psalms, concerning me." And again the evangelist makes a significant and momentous addition, "Then opened he their understanding, that they might understand the scriptures."

Here we have the Biblical warrant for the Biblical teaching that predictive prophecy is not only a feature, but an outstanding and unique element in the religion of the Bible. It consists in the words of the Lord Himself and of His Apostles. If, then, a belief in the fulfilment of prophecy is due to a method of interpretation which is either "open to question" or "obviously false," what is there in the teachings of the New Testament upon which the Christian can confidently rely?[25] If Paul's argument for the reality and meaning of the 'death of Christ and His glorious resurrection is either questionable or obviously false in so far as it appeals to the Old Testament, what reason is there to believe that his appeal to the living witnesses is any more dependable?

Let us not deceive ourselves. If the Biblical evidence for predictive prophecy is set aside as undependable, then instead of placing our confidence in what the Christian Church has throughout the centuries regarded as "a sure word of prophecy, to which all will do well that they give heed" the Christian of today who accepts the "critical" conception of prophecy is shut up to the solution of a "difficult philosophical problem," a problem which can find its answer, if indeed it can be called an answer, only in the vague and tantalizing phraseology of Platonic myth. He is shut up to "stories" (myths) which are quite likely to be untrue or at best only partly true. Yet the Apostle Peter emphatically repudiates the comparison of the glorious facts and precious promises of the Gospel with "cunningly devised fables" ("sophisticated myths," cf. the Greek of 2 Pet. 1:16). It may be regarded as certain that Paul and probably Peter were familiar with the word "myth" as used in the lofty and worthy sense which we have been considering. If so, it is significant that both of them use it only in the low and ignoble sense which it had long since acquired. For, as Trench has pointed out, the words "word" (logos) and "myth" (muthos) were originally lofty words which differed but little in meaning. But the difference "grew ever wider and wider until in the end a great gulf has separated them each from the other," because they came to belong, "one to the kingdom of light and truth, the other to that of darkness and lies."[26] This is the gulf that separates the "word of truth" as made known through prophets and apostles and through the Incarnate Word from the myths and legends of paganism, be they ever so cultured and refined. It is tragic that there should be today Christian scholars who are turning to pagan myths to justify and vindicate, in the case of one of the most precious passages of the Old Testament, a "sure word of prophecy" which, because of their acceptance of an unscriptural theory regarding prophecy, they can no longer regard as sure.

---

[25] Professor Burrows rejects the idea of external authority. He holds that "the only sound criterion for determining whether anything is an authentic revelation is its intrinsic value" and that we must accept the principle that "what is ultimately authoritative for us is that which commands the assent of our own best judgment, accepted as the witness of the Spirit within us" (op. cit., p. 50). That this is something quite different from the testimonium Spiritus sancti to the truth of the Scriptures is quite obvious. For according to this author the Bible contains many errors of fact and interpretation.

[26] Synonyms of the New Testament, § xc.

CONCLUSION

The aim of this brief study of the subject of Prophecy has been to direct attention to two matters which are of the utmost importance in dealing with the problem of the Unity of Isaiah. The first of these is that the unity of Isaiah finds clear and adequate support in the evidence furnished by the Bible as a whole as to the true nature of Prophecy. According to this evidence, prediction formed an important part of the message of the prophets. They spoke, it is true, of things present, but they also spoke, frequently and impressively, of things to come. And when they spoke of the future, they sometimes spoke of its events as future; at other times they spoke of things to come as if they were living among them and as if the scenes of which they spoke were being enacted before their very eyes. *The almost unanimous acceptance during twenty-five centuries of the Isaianic authorship of the entire Book of Isaiah can be adequately and fully accounted for only by the fact that such a view of it is fully in accord with the conception of Prophecy set forth in the Bible as a whole.* And this explanation is confirmed by the further fact that it was not until another and radically different conception of prophecy began to gain acceptance with critics of the Bible —a theory which insisted on confining prophecy more or less completely to contemporary events with a view to eliminating the predictive element from it—that the unity of Isaiah was seriously questioned and finally utterly rejected by them. Such a view of prophecy must of necessity destroy the unity of Isaiah, but—and this must never be forgotten—it must first recast, remodel, and all but destroy the entire structure of Biblical prophecy of which Isaiah 40-66 forms only a part, though a most important one. In other words, Biblical prophecy and the unity of Isaiah stand or fall together!

The second point which has been stressed is that the whole question of *Messianic* prophecy, of a New Testament fulfilment of Old Testament predictions, is involved and is at stake in the problem of the unity of Isaiah. The claim that Isaiah 40-66 must date from the time of Cyrus because Cyrus is represented as the contemporary of the prophet has as its necessary corollary the conclusion that the Suffering Servant of Isa. 53 was also a contemporary of the prophet who describes him so vividly. For it cannot be successfully maintained that the one figure is more vividly present to the eye of the prophet than is the other. If

122

then the prophet is thinking and speaking of a contemporary, as the thoroughly consistent among the critics do not hesitate to insist, there is logically no room for a Messianic interpretation and a New Testament fulfilment of this wonderful prediction of the Suffering Servant, which is so precious to multitudes of Christians, because they believe that it speaks so plainly of One who has borne their sins upon the Cross and risen victorious over death for their justification. The meaning placed on the words "situation" and "scope" by the critics makes it difficult for them—it really makes it impossible for them—to find for a prophecy uttered by an Old Testament prophet regarding a contemporary a real fulfilment in the New Testament.

Since the Cyrus Prophecies have figured so prominently in the attempt to prove the critical theory of two or more Isaiahs, the problem of the correct interpretation of these prophecies has called for particular attention. The aim has been to show that while Cyrus is at times referred to with a vividness which suggests that the prophet was speaking of and to a contemporary, the prophet has at the same time made it quite clear by means of a poem which exhibits a remarkable chronological emphasis and gives every indication of very careful design, that Cyrus belongs to the distant future. If this be so, the Cyrus Prophecies themselves may properly be regarded as constituting a remarkable confirmation of the time-honored and we believe thoroughly Biblical belief that "Isaiah the son of Amoz was the author of every part of the book that goes under his name."

In this study of the Unity of Isaiah, the discussion has been largely confined to the two great figures, Cyrus and the Suffering Servant. But it is to be remembered that the great burden of this wonderful book is Messianic and eschatological. And this major theme runs through the whole of it. The vision of the glory of the "last days" meets us already in 2:2-4. It is enlarged upon in 11:1-9. It is the great theme of chaps. 24-27, which mention among other things the conquest of death, the "last enemy," (25:8; cf. 1 Cor. 15:26, 54). And finally it speaks of the "new heavens and the new earth" (65:17; 66:22), thus supplying the theme for the glorious picture of the Holy City with which the Book of Revelation closes (chaps. 21-22). The Revelation is in many respects a difficult book to interpret. But its great central theme is unmistakably plain. It is the certain and final triumph of the kingdom of God, the Church, the Bride of the Lamb. This theme reaches its climax in the burst of Alleluias in chap. 19 which ends with those words of triumph: "Alleluia: for the Lord God Omnipotent reigneth." This is all predictive prophecy. The Alleluias are sung not by the Church Militant but by the Church Triumphant. It is with these glory songs, that the Christian Church has comforted herself in her darkest hours of persecution and suffering and defeat, assured that soon or late, how soon she cannot tell, "the night of weeping shall be the morn of song." For "the mouth of the Lord hath spoken it."

It cannot be too strongly emphasized that all the hopes of the Christian, both for this world and the next, rest on the promises of God as they are made known in the Scriptures. These promises are great and exceeding precious. But if these promises are dependable and sure, then they are predictions. They are a sure word of prophecy. They concern things to come. And these promises are not only exceeding precious, they are also practical, challenging, and inspiring. Jesus said to His disciples: "All power is given unto me in heaven and in earth. Go ye therefore, and teach all nations, baptizing them in the name of the Father, and of the Son, and of the Holy Ghost; teaching them to observe all things whatsoever I have commanded you; and, lo, I am with you alway, *even* unto the end of the world. Amen."

Why are the hearts of Christians failing them for fear in these difficult and dangerous post-war days? Is it because they have no sure word of Prophecy to guide them? If so, is this because they have been giving heed to those who tell them that the most definite and positive statements of the Bible are not to be trusted, but are to be set aside if they fail to agree with the "assured results" of rationalistic Higher Criticism? Is it because they have allowed those who are wise in the wisdom of the world to deprive them of the glorious and gracious promises of the Word of God? Is it because the great and oft-repeated argument of Isa. 40-48 that the God of Israel proves His sole and unique Deity by the fact that He can and does both predict and fulfil has lost its cogency because it raises the "difficult philosophical problem" whether there can be an actual prevision of future events? If so, they will do well to give heed to the words of the son of Amoz: "To the law and to the testimony: if they speak not according to this word, it is because there is no light in them" (8:20) and "The grass withereth and the flower fadeth: but the word of our God shall stand for ever" (40:8)— words which join the two parts of Isaiah together and which also find their fullest confirmation in the words of Him who said of the Old Covenant: "Till heaven and earth pass, one jot or one tittle shall in no wise pass from the law, till all be fulfilled" (Matt. 6:18), and of the New Covenant: "Heaven and earth shall pass away but my words shall not pass away" (24:35). A Church which rests securely on the Bible as the Word of God and gives earnest heed to the challenge and the promise of the Great Commission need have no fear for the future, however dark and threatening that future may seem to be. She need not be appalled by the onward march of totalitarian Communism or of equally totalitarian Romanism. She may claim the promise: "five of you shall chase an hundred, and an hundred of you shall put ten thousand to flight" (Lev. 26:8). But if the Church loses through unbelief her grasp on that sword of the Spirit which is the Word of God, if she allows it to rust in its scabbard through disuse, if she allows it to be dulled and nicked and broken through sceptical attack, she may well fear that those other words of Isaiah will be true of her, "One thousand *shall flee* at the rebuke of one" (30:17). For the mouth of the Lord hath spoken it.

APPENDIX

I

In this discussion of prophecy the word "predict" is used in its ordinary sense of *foretell*. The prefix *pre* (Latin *prae*), like the *pro* in Greek, may have both local and temporal force. Hence the "prophet" (*prophētēs*) may be both one who forthtells, i.e., who speaks for or interprets another, as Aaron was Moses' prophet (Ex. 7:1, cf. 4:15f.), or one who foretells things to come (Deut. 18:21f.). This is admirably stated in the Davis *Dictionary of the Bible* (4th. ed., 1924, p. 625): "The English word is derived from the Greek *prophētēs* which means one who speaks for another, an interpreter or proclaimer, and one who speaks beforehand, a predictor. This twofold meaning is due to the two senses of the preposition *pro*, for and before." In the "Revised and Rewritten" edition of this Dictionary (published as *The Westminster Dictionary of the Bible* in 1944), on the basis of the classical usage of the word, the second meaning is all but eliminated and we are told: "The *prophētēs*, accordingly, is not a predictor, but one who speaks forth that which he has received from the divine Spirit. The prefix *pro* is not temporal. The prophet speaks for, or in behalf of another; he is the mouthpiece or the spokesman of God." To this definite and unqualified statement the further sentence is added: "He is a forthteller rather than a foreteller" (p. 493), which suggests that the difference is after all not absolute but relative. Whatever may be said of the classical usage, which is of course the pagan usage, it is quite clear that the statement in the *Davis Dictionary* correctly represents the *Biblical* usage. For in the Bible the idea of foretelling is so closely connected with the function of the prophet that it is impossible to believe that the temporal force of the *pro* should be ignored or denied. The first revelation made to Samuel was a *fore*telling of the doom of Eli's house, which Samuel at once *forth*told to Eli; and it was because the Lord did not allow any of Samuel's words to "fall to the ground," i.e., to fail of fulfilment, that all Israel knew that Samuel was established to be a prophet of the Lord (1 Sam. 3:11-21). Similarly in Acts 2:30f. Peter speaks of David as a "prophet" and, by virtue of this fact, as "foreseeing" (*proidōn*) the resurrection of Christ. Here the *pro* is certainly temporal. It would be absurd to render by "forthseeing," which shows how arbitrary it is, to

126

say the least, to insist that the *pro-* of prophet must be restricted to the local sense. This attempt of the critics to eliminate the idea of *fore*telling from the word "prophet" indicates very clearly how averse they are to the admission that foretelling was an important element in prophecy.

II

The above quotations from the writings of A. B. Davidson are both appropriate and inappropriate. They are appropriate because Davidson was a leader in developing and popularizing the "critical" theory regarding prophecy which is so widely held today. As professor at New College, Edinburgh, for nearly forty years (1863-1902), he taught many generations of theological students, among whom were Wm. Robertson Smith and George Adam Smith; and his lectures on Prophecy exerted a powerful influence on theological thinking throughout the English-speaking world. The words which we have quoted express clearly and concisely the two great principles which dominate the theory of prophecy which his teaching and writings did so much to popularize: the emphasis on the *situation* of the prophet and the limiting of the *scope* of his prophecies.

The inappropriateness consists in the fact that Davidson was not at all consistent in the carrying out of the principles which he stated at times so clearly and forcefully. In a review of Davidson's lectures on *The Theology of the Old Testament,* which like his lectures on *Old Testament Prophecy* were published shortly after his death, the late Professor Geerhardus Vos of Princeton, pointed out that Davidson occupied "an intermediate position, which, in our opinion, does justice to neither the old nor the modern view and is, on account of its continual oscillation between the two, weaker than either of them" (*Princeton Theol. Review,* vol. iv., p. 116). This is no less true of the *Lectures on Prophecy.* In this very fact we have striking proof of the difficulty, we would better say impossibility, of bridging the gap between the traditional view of prophecy which Davidson rejected and the critical view of which he became a vigorous advocate. This is indicated especially clearly by his attitude to the question of prediction, the problem of the future. The first statement quoted seems to indicate quite definitely that in the utterances of the prophets the future, certainly the distant future, can have figured very little. The second statement, which seems to indicate that Davidson would have liked to disregard the predictive element completely had this been possible, is qualified by saying that prediction was resorted to "only on moral grounds" or "oftener to break up in the stormy cloud a rift through which the shining peaceful heaven could be seen beyond" (p. 11), which obviously makes large concessions to the conservative position. Elsewhere he describes "its outlook into the future" as "just the characteristic of the religion of Israel" (p. 59); and he even goes so far as to say, "And, indeed, the future was what the prophets lived in" (p. 83). He finds in prophecy both a "Messianic" and an "eschatological" element. Yet unless prediction enters very definitely into the definition of prophecy, these words become practically meaningless. He speaks of a New Testament "fulfilment" of Old Testament prophecy. Yet *fulfilment* and *prediction* are correlative words each of which is meaningless and certainly valueless without the other. He does not hesitate to say: "There must be a connection between prophecy and fulfilment" (p. 377). Obviously there must. And if in prophecy we have the *foretelling* of things to come, then the connection between prophecy and fulfilment is not far to seek nor difficult to find. But when the element of prediction is greatly curtailed or denied, the connection between the two, if indeed there be any, tends to disappear; and the task of establishing a real nexus between them becomes, when this attenuated view of prophecy is adopted, not only a major problem for the critical student of prophecy, but one which is impossible of solution.

III

It is a little more than a century since Joseph Addison Alexander published his two-volume Commentary on Isaiah (1846-7). It was a work of massive scholarship; and its appearance marked an epoch, at least in America, in the interpretation of Old Testament prophecy. It is still of great value for the following reasons: (1) it defends the unity of the entire book on the basis of such a conception of prophecy as can alone justify it and make its acceptance possible; viz. the hearty acceptance of the view that prophecy is essentially supernatural and that the element of prediction figures prominently in it and is to be recognized, emphasized, and rejoiced in. (2) It does this only after giving careful consideration to opposing viewpoints, and to the history of interpretation with which Alexander was thoroughly acquainted. Alexander was no obscurantist. He knew the views of his opponents quite as well as his own! (3) It shows the reader that there has been relatively little change in the course of a century in the position of those who reject the unity of Isaiah. Basically their position is the same as it was a hundred years ago. For these three reasons "Alexander on Isaiah" is still very valuable and remarkably up-to-date.

As to the rejection of *predictive* prophecy Alexander does not hesitate to say:

"This is the fundamental doctrine of the modern neological interpreters, the *foregone conclusion,* to which all exegetical results must yield or be accommodated, and in support of which the arbitrary processes before described must be employed for the discovery of arguments, philological, historical, rhetorical, moral, against the genuineness of the passage, which might just as easily be used in other cases, where they are dispensed with, simply because they are not needed for the purpose of destroying an explicit proof of inspiration." (vol. i.xxxviii)

These words were penned a hundred years ago. They are as true today and as applicable to the present situation as if the ink had not yet dried on the page on which they were written.

Alexander also makes it clear that the way in which the critics usually approach this subject is not by a flat and outspoken rejection of the supernatural as such, but by means of their conception of the *situation* and *scope* of the prophecy. Thus he tells us regarding chaps. 40-66:

"The first and main objection to the doctrine that Isaiah wrote these chapters, although variously stated by the writers who have urged it, is in substance this: that the Prophet everywhere alludes to the circumstances and events of the Babylonian Exile as those by which he was himself surrounded and with which he was familiar, from which his conceptions and his images are borrowed, and out of which he looks both at the future and the past, and in the midst of which he must as a necessary consequence have lived and written" (vol. ii., p. xix).

Here we have as clear a statement as could be asked for of that argument from "situation" of which present day criticism makes so much.

As to the "assumption that the local and historical allusions of a prophet must be always those of his own time," meaning that the prophet cannot deal with a non-existent situation, Alexander points out that this is a question-begging assumption, since it assumes the very thing that is to be proved. He holds it to be an assumption that is refuted by "the analogy of other kinds of composition, in which all grant that a writer may assume a '*Standpunkt*' different from his own, and personate those earlier and later than himself." He points out that the "classical historians" have done this, that it is the method used by "dramatic poets," and by "still more imaginative writers, when they throw themselves into the future, and surround themselves by circumstances not yet in existence." Then he remarks: "If it be natural for poets thus to speak of an ideal future, why may not prophets of a real one?" To this he replies, "The only answer is, *because they cannot know it;* and to this point all the tortuous evasions of the more reserved neologists as surely tend as the positive averments of their bolder brethren. In every form, this argument against the genuineness of the book before us is at bottom a denial of prophetic inspiration as impossible" (vol. ii, p. xx).

"Another erroneous supposition," according to Alexander, is that the utterances of the Prophets must have been intended "solely for the contemporaries of the writer," and that "the Babylonian exile is the subject of the whole book." Here he deals with the critical argument regarding the *scope* of prophecy. "The prophet's work, according to this theory, is more confined than that of the orator or poet. These may be said to labour for posterity; but his views must be limited to those about him." The majority of the critics, according to Alexander "appear to be agreed that nothing could be more absurd than consolation under sorrows which were not to be experienced for ages." His answer is an impressive one.

"If the book, as we have reason to believe, was intended to secure a suc-cession of the highest ends,—the warning and instruction of the Prophet's own contemporaries, the encouragement and consolation of the pious exiles, the reproof and conviction of their unbelieving brethren, the engagement of the Persians and especially of Cyrus in the service of Jehovah, the vindication of God's dealings with the Jews both in wrath and mercy, and a due preparation of the minds of true believers for the advent of Messiah,—then such objections as the one last cited must be either unmeaning and impertinent, or simply equivalent to a denial of prophetic inspiration" (vol. ii, p. xxi).

These few quotations may serve to convince the reader that "Alexander on Isaiah" is by no means out-of-date, despite the fact that the critics are disposed to ignore him. To commemorate the centennial of the appearance of this commentary and also with a view to pointing out the permanent value of Alexander's contribution to the study of Isaiah, Professor E. J. Young of Westminster Theological Seminary has published (1946-48) a series of three Articles on "The Study of Isaiah since the Time of Joseph Addison Alexander" (*Westminster Theol. Journal,* Vols. ix. pp. 1-30, x. 23-56, 139-67). Writing from the standpoint of one who heartily shares Alexander's basic position, Young discusses the course of a century of "critical" interpretation of Isaiah which has studiously ignored him and points out the necessity of a return to that Biblical conception of Prophecy of which Alexander was so able an exponent.

IV

The words, "young woman old enough for marriage" imply, unless the chastity of the young woman is called in question that the mother of this child is a married young woman. Davidson admitted that the word used here is "apparently always used of unmarried women" (*op. cit.* p. 361), which means that it is always used of women who are or ought to be virgins. The clearest example of such usage is furnished by Gen. 24, where Rebekah, who is introduced in v. 16 as "a virgin [*bethulah*], neither had any man known her," is in v. 43 simply called "a virgin" (*almah,* the word used in Isa. 7:14). For a "young woman" who is married to bear a son is a natural and ordinary event, as well as a joyous and blessed one. For a "virgin" to bear a son is something quite different; it is extraordinary, it is supernatural. Davidson admitted that Isaiah's offer to Ahaz of a "sign" indicated that "Isaiah was prepared to give Ahaz something miraculous" (p. 360). He felt also that the rendering "virgin" (*parthenos*) of the Greek (LXX), a rendering which is followed in Matt. 1:24, "may be considered in some sense providential" (p. 359). Yet the sentence quoted above in part reads in full as follows: "But probably the word [*almah*], though apparently always used of an unmarried woman, means properly an adult young woman." This means that while Davidson was prepared to admit that the Biblical use of the word justifies and supports the rendering "virgin," he nevertheless preferred the rendering "young woman." He tells us that there is reason to regard the birth as miraculous; and he also tells us that the rendering is to be rejected which makes it so. It is this "intermediate position," as Dr. Vos called it, between the old and the new views of prophecy which we meet constantly in Davidson and in many of his numerous followers, which makes their statements so unsatisfactory and often so misleading. They use such words as "prediction" and "fulfilment," while at the same time advocating a theory of prophecy which tends to empty both words of their true meaning.

V

The integrity of the text of Isaiah 44:24-28 has been attacked in recent years mainly on two grounds.

(1) The Metrical Form of the Poem. The modern study of Metrics as applied to the Old Testament poetry goes back to Julius Ley who in 1875 published an elaborate study of the

subject. Ley confined his attention almost entirely to the Psalms and Lamentations. Among the numerous metres which he recognized was the "elegiac pentameter," so called because of its frequent occurrence in the Book of Lamentations. Subsequent writers have called it the *Qinah* (i.e., "lamentation") verse. It consists of a line which has five accented syllables, and which is divided by a "caesura" into two parts or members, the first having three accents, the second two. Budde (1882) appears to have been the first to discover this metre in the Prophets (Isa. 45:14-25). In a subsequent study (1891), in dealing with the Cyrus prophecy, he divided 44:23-28 into fourteen *Qinah* lines, all but two of which could be regarded as complete. The defective lines were: "that spreadeth abroad the earth: who was with me" and, "That saith of Jerusalem she shall be inhabited." These he regarded as representing the first members of two defective lines. This made the recovery of the original form of these lines the special task of the Metricists.

According to the view which has now been widely adopted by critics (e.g. Duhm, Cheyne, Marti) vv. 24-28 constitute a *Qinah* poem of two stanzas, each having five lines. The following arrangement allowing for minor variations, is the one which is generally accepted:

"Thus-saith Yahweh, thy-Redeemer and-thy-Fashioner from-the-womb.
I-am Yahweh, that-created-all-things that-stretched-out the-heaven
I-alone, that-grounded the-earth who with-me?
That-destroys the-signs of-mantics and-diviners he-makes-fools
That-turns the wise backward and-makes-folly their-wisdom

That-establishes the-word of-his-serv- and-the-counsel of-his-messengers
ant [he performs]
He-that-saith of-J. let-it-be-inhabited [and-of-the-temple, be-founded]
And-of-the-ruins of-the-land, let-them and-their-ruins I-will-build-up
be-built
He-that-saith to-the-Deep, Dry-up and-thy-streams I-dry-up
He-that-saith of-Cyrus, my-shepherd and[-all]-my-pleasure he-fulfils."

This arrangement involves four modifications or changes in the text of the poem: (1) By transferring the "alone" to the following clause the "who-was with-me?" can be regarded as a very abbreviated second member of the third line. (2) By transferring the last clause of v. 28 "and of the temple, be-founded" to form the second member of the sixth line, that line is completed. This involves the elision of the words which precede it, "and-of-the-cities of-Judah they-shall-be-built," as a duplicate of the first part of line 8. (3) By dropping out the "he-performs" of line 6 the second member is reduced to two accents. (4) By dropping the "all" from line 10 the words, "and-my-pleasure he-shall-perform," are likewise reduced to the two accents required for the second member of a *Qinah* line.

If the reader will compare the above arrangement with the Climactic, he will note that the advocates of the *Qinah* arrangement find difficulty in carrying it through just where such difficulty would naturally arise if the climactic arrangement is the correct one. The second strophe can of course be regarded as forming three *Qinah* lines, especially if the words "he-performeth" are cut away from the last line, or "the counsel of his messengers" is reduced to "his counsel." The main difficulty is with the first and the last strophes. The first strophe consists of three single members. The problem is to form two *Qinah* lines (i.e. four members) out of it. This is accomplished in part by taking the words "I am Jehovah" and making them begin the second line of the *Qinah* poem. This is a very radical change because it deprives these words of their commanding position as the great affirmation, the significance of which all of the nine participial clauses that follow are intended, in a sense, merely to illustrate. Even then the third line is clumsy and weak. The "alone" belongs with what precedes it and the "Who (-was) with-me?" is really too weak to form the second member of the line. But the greatest difficulty is with the third strophe. This strophe has a total of *nine members*. Four *Qinah* lines would have only eight. So one of the nine must be gotten rid of. The simplest way to do this is to treat the words of the third member of the last line of this strophe, "even-to-say of-Jerusalem she-shall-be-built" as a "doublet" of the second member of the first line, "That-saith of-Jerusalem she-shall-be-built." If it is deleted, then the last member of the same line, "and-(of-the-)temple: thy-foundation-shall-be-laid," can be added to the first member of the first line; and the second and third members of that line can be regarded as constituting a complete *Qinah* line. In this way two *Qinah* lines are made out of the first line of the strophe and the last member of the third line; and the third line is reduced to a single *Qinah* line. To those who are accustomed to think in terms of "doublets" and to seek for them as proof of corruption of the text, such a change in the third strophe may seem very minor and eminently proper. But it is utterly destructive of the beauty and symmetry of the poem. No textual evidence has been cited in support of it. It is purely conjectural. Contrast with all this the fact that the climactic arrangement does not require the slightest change in the text! This fact should indicate very clearly the superiority of the climactic arrangement.

(2) A more radical attack upon this verse is that made by C. C. Torrey (*The Second Isaiah*, 1928). In the endeavor to eliminate "Babylonian" features from chaps. xl-lv, he challenged the genuineness of all of the five references to Cyrus which he found in these chapters. His view was accepted by G. A. Barton (*Haverford Symposium* [1938] p. 61) who admitted, however, that it had not proved acceptable "to the great majority of scholars." W. A. L. Elmslie (*How Came Our Faith?*, [1949] p. 342) vigorously seconds Torrey. He declares: "Torrey is on immensely strong ground in judging them to be glosses. The pivotal point is the equation of Cyrus with God's chosen and anointed servant." This Elmslie regards as "not credible." In support of his claim that "In xlv. 1 *to Cyrus* was surely no part of the original text," he adds this illuminating footnote: "In the immediately preceding verse (xliv. 28), which is the last verse in ch. xliv, *Cyrus* is also named. But (before Torrey wrote on the subject) this verse had been recognized as secondary, a 'tag-on' to the chapter, redundant after *v.* 26 and inconsistent with the tenor of the context. Moreover, *Cyrus* is not found in the LXX text. The sole relevant question concerns *Cyrus* in xlv. 1." This is a surprising statement. The name *Cyrus* appears in v. 28 in the Sinaitic and Vatican mss. of the LXX and in the Chester Beatty Papyrus. The reason Elmslie suspects v. 28 is not on textual, but purely subjective and conjectural grounds.

INDEX OF AUTHORS

INDEX OF AUTHORS

Made in the USA
Monee, IL
13 July 2023

39172278R00088